NORWICH

EIGHTY YEARS OF
THE NORWICH SOCIETY

BRITAIN

IN OLD PHOTOGRAPHS

NORWICH

EIGHTY YEARS OF
THE NORWICH SOCIETY

A.P. ANDERSON & NEIL R. STOREY

SUTTON PUBLISHING

Sutton Publishing Limited
Phoenix Mill · Thrupp · Stroud
Gloucestershire · GL5 2BU

First published 2004

Copyright ©
A.P. Anderson & Neil R. Storey, 2004

Title page photograph: Orford Place, *c.* 1900.

British Library Cataloguing in Publication Data
A catalogue record for this book is available from the
British Library.

ISBN 0-7509-3377-1

Typeset in 10.5/13.5 Photina.
Typesetting and origination by
Sutton Publishing Limited.
Printed and bound in England by
J.H. Haynes & Co. Ltd, Sparkford.

*This book is dedicated to all members of the Norwich Society,
past and present, and especially to the memory of
Philip Hepworth and Jean Ogden*

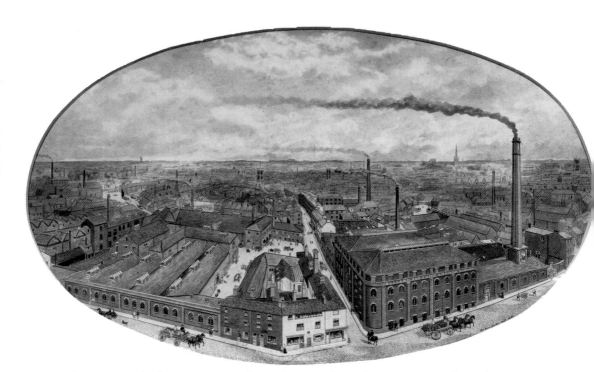

A view over the late Victorian industrial city, with Anchor Brewery to the right, *c.* 1888.
(Allan Sewell)

CONTENTS

The view across the old cattle market, complete with stock pens and passing window cleaners, *c.* 1925. This photograph has caught the atmosphere of a Norwich which has now passed for ever, and is only truly captured in writing by those who knew it so well, such as Ralph Mottram in *If Stones Could Speak* or 'Jonathan Mardle' in his *Wednesday Mornings* essays.

FOREWORD

My first reaction upon reading this book was to reflect upon the debt present and future citizens of Norwich owe to the energy, commitment and foresight of the leadership of the Norwich Society. During the past eighty years the Society has cajoled, threatened, campaigned and shown the way with new ideas and exemplary projects. It has clearly played a significant part in ensuring that Norwich has now one of the best planned and interesting city centres of its size in the country.

The battle between preservation and progress is a second thread which weaves its way through the Society's history. Social, economic and political forces for change have made their impact upon the physical fabric of the city. The lessons of recent history show that this change must not be rushed. There is merit in caution. Too often the knife has been put into the heart of historic centres only to regret the action many years on.

The book also traces the relationship between the local council and the Norwich Society. The early years of the Society were marked by antagonism; in most recent times the atmosphere has been one of cooperation and support. The decision in 1959 to make the Lord Mayor the president of the Society has no doubt helped, but perhaps, too, the realisation that deep conflict helps neither side, nor the city. With global economic forces constantly threatening local distinctiveness, unity of purpose between local council and civic society is essential.

My final thought is that all in all Norwich has not done too badly. For the future, one hopes the city will continue to afford much greater priority to pedestrians than vehicles, make creative use of its riverside, and encourage outstanding contemporary buildings, such as the Forum. There is potential too to unite the city's heritage, which has been saved, into a powerful force for social and economic good, and to spread the high standards of the city centre's environment to surrounding suburbs and estates. Indeed, one can be sure life will not stand still, as this book shows, and that the Society too will have to adapt. Its lasting challenge is to broaden its appeal to all ages and groups so that its caring values for the well being and fabric of Norwich, which have served the city well for the past eighty years, are shared by all. I wish the future leadership of the Society and Norwich itself every success.

Martin Bacon
Chief Executive, Civic Trust

The Curat House. Situated in a small courtyard behind Backs on the Haymarket, this ancient building was a popular meeting place and restaurant in the city. It was here that the founders of the Norwich Society gathered for their first meeting on 23 March 1923.

INTRODUCTION

Civic societies play a larger part in our lives than is often realised, and their role in the life of a city, town or village is not always understood or appreciated. Not possessed of statutory powers, they must be persuasive in character and depend for their effectiveness upon the good sense and consistency of their views. They possess one considerable advantage in that they come to the forum of local

...e view across Theatre Street from the Assembly House, *c.* 1901. The only building left standing today is ...e church of St Peter Mancroft, seen on the right of the photograph.

The city of Norwich viewed from the castle mound in the late nineteenth century. In the immediate foreground is the cattle market and horse sale ground while in the distance is Peafield Mill, New Lakenham. As the city approached the twentieth century many of the squalid tenements were demolished and replaced with new, impressive buildings designed by notable architects like George Skipper. Residential accommodation was spreading confidently beyond the city walls and the new transport scheme of tramways would change the face of Norwich for ever.

debate unhampered by vested interest. Societies vary a great deal in size and in the length of their existence, but they have one thing in common: they are composed of people who care very much for the place in which they live or work, or with which they have ties of affection and regard.

It is not difficult to imagine Norwich in the period after the First World War, a crowded place, full of churches and narrow streets, with its people trying to adjust to the losses and privations the war had brought, and hoping for better things. Neither is it hard to understand the growing voice, soon to make itself felt in political change, that called for a sweeping away of the old, the inadequate dwellings in the 'yards' and the generally poor sanitary arrangements. Spirit and vitality were there but people wanted more. 'Let's do away with all this and give the people something decent' was the feeling of the day. It took courage and tenacity to temper such a

e view across the city from the castle mound in the late twentieth century. Gone almost without a trace
e all vestiges of the cattle market, and most of the buildings in the row immediately beyond disappeared in
e course of the Castle Mall development. Great concrete and glass structures fill the view at all levels, but
ll the integrity of the city as a whole remains. Although the lush city of orchards or city in orchard as
scribed by Fuller may not remain today, it is still a treasure of greenery and historic buildings.
arah Cocke)

powerful sentiment, but that was the task undertaken by the founders of the
Norwich Society. These citizens were not against change; indeed from its earliest
days the Society proclaimed its faith both in renewal and preservation. What was
needed in the early 1920s was to understand that in Norwich buildings entirely
worthy of a provincial capital very often walked hand-in-hand with squalor, and that
one must not be sacrificed in dealing with the other. Therefore the first task was to
obtain recognition for things of value within the old city, and then to seek their
preservation. It is easy to forget, eighty years on, the threats to buildings that today
we take for granted.

The Norwich Society has reached a significant milestone, and it can now look
back over the eighty years during which it has tried to be a reasonable and
responsible voice, always seeking to preserve what is best in an old English city, not

Orford Place, *c.* 1900. Wooden scaffolding props and poster-plastered hoardings on the buildings, c
through from Orford Place to Castle Meadow. These new cuts and roadways for the new tram syste
opened on 30 July 1900. Stretching for 19 miles in and around the city, the tram routes were the me
significant changes to the structure of the city since medieval times.

short of beauty or architectural and historic interest. It has also sought the very best
of the new, not regarding the city as one large museum but a vital place playing
several roles – historic city, provincial capital and an economic, social, and cultural
centre of importance. Norwich can very obviously not stand still, nor has it done so
in eighty years. The Norwich Society has tried to ensure that change, in whatever
form, has not been to the detriment of the essential character of the city. Each of the
eight decades of its existence has presented different challenges to the Society and
the city itself. To describe how those challenges have been met is the purpose of this
book.

1

The 1920s

The Founders Assemble –
Early Successes

Norwich city market place complete with trams and policeman on point duty in
front of Jarrold's Corner, *c.* 1925. The buildings to the right behind the market,
many of them old pubs, had gradually been bought by the City Council to become
municipal offices. By the 1930s the warren of buildings had become impractical,
not to mention rat-infested, and all were demolished to make way for the new
City Hall and market place opened in 1938.

The period between the two world wars was a high point for local government in Norwich. The desire for change was matched by the will to carry improvements forward. People became involved in local affairs to get things done, and in Norwich there was plenty to do. To read the minutes of Norwich Corporation for this period is to understand the measure of the achievement: one clearance order after another was issued as people were moved to better conditions, from the old city to the comparative wonders of the new estates. With the perspective of hindsight, one can understand everything the Corporation was trying to do. Its concern was for the city's people and their needs. That the authorities were wary of this new Society, whose members did not live in difficult conditions and who appeared to want to thwart the Corporation's good intentions, is not to be wondered at. On the other hand, those who had come together to form the Norwich Society were certainly not scornful of the Corporation's aspirations; rather, they thought that something beyond improved living conditions was necessary. The city had to retain a quality and a character that made it a place in which people would wish to live.

The late Philip Hepworth has well described that first meeting of architects and members of the Norfolk and Norwich Archaeological Society under the chairmanship of Edward Boardman at the Curat House on 23 March 1923 that brought the Norwich Society into being. A man who saw the imminent danger of the city losing buildings of value was Walter Randall Rudd (1852–1927), a wine merchant in Castle Meadow. Rudd had other business interests, was widely travelled and was long associated with the Archaeological Society. In 1919 he had told that Society's Council of the 'threatened destruction of ancient buildings in Norwich' and of the need for 'influential members and citizens interested' to meet and consider the matter. Such concerns were brought into sharp focus by a proposal to widen the medieval Bishop Bridge. It was a colleague of Rudd's in the Archaeological Society, described by Hepworth as an 'antiquarian solicitor', Basil Cozens-Hardy, who proposed that the Curat House meeting should take place.

The Society rapidly placed the day-to-day affairs in the hands of a sub-committee. Its members included Rudd and Cozens-Hardy; Major S.E. Glendenning, an engineer; Stanley J. Wearing, an architect; Helen C. Colman, who was later that year to act as Lady Mayoress to her sister Ethel; E.W.B. Scott of the firm A.F. Scott and Sons; and the Society's secretary, Arthur Batchelor. Batchelor, who lived in Bracondale, was an artist of quality, educated at Wellington, Oxford and the Slade. Hepworth described him as a 'man of many interests slightly detached from the main concerns of the Norwich Society', and saw this as a good thing as the secretary was expected to be 'a recorder of, not a participant in, the business of those he served'.

In May 1923 the Society met to hear J.P. Bushe-Fox of the then Ministry of Works speak on the procedures for listing suitable buildings and on the work of the Society for the Protection of Ancient Buildings. Emboldened by this, by October of that year the sub-committee had drawn up a list of structures seen as worthy of listing. As well as the castle, with its precincts and buildings adjacent to the cathedral, the sub-committee looked at buildings within the historic great wards of the city and 'the county of the city' (that area of the city outside the walls but inside the boundary). In Conesford Ward Howard House and 'the Carrow Ruins' were considered, and in Mancroft the Guildhall, the Curat House and the Assembly House. In Wymer Ward, it was Gybson's Well, the Bridewell, 'the old gateway adjoining Augustine's Steward's house', and St Andrew's Hall, 'the Dutch Church and adjoining monastic buildings', and the Great Hospital cloister. In 'Over the Water', Bacon House and Whitefriars' Bridge were added; and in the county of the city, Magdalen Chapel (the Lazar House) and Hardley Cross. A submission was made to the Ministry and a great start was made in preserving the city's architectural treasures.

There were successes and failures. Work on Bishop Bridge was stopped and the structure listed. Pull's Ferry and the Erpingham and Ethelbert gates were scheduled, but the efforts to stop the demolition of the medieval Whitefriar's Bridge failed. The battle began to save Elm Hill, particularly the north side that was threatened with demolition. The sub-committee was unceasing in its work. Castle Meadow was being widened and the City Council had agreed to the construction of a new county police headquarters near the Shirehall that would have destroyed much of the garden surrounding the Castle. Representations brought about a rethink and the police moved elsewhere. The Society had done something 'to make the weather'. The Corporation acted upon a suggestion from the Society for the Protection of Ancient Buildings and set up an Ancients Buildings Committee, with the Society being granted six of the fourteen seats. This was too good to last. One councillor thought the committee had delayed slum clearance; others that the Society 'wished to preserve slums and to oppose all alterations involving the destruction of anything old'. Earlier there had been a better relationship with the council, with the Society praising the 'splendid work' in repairing the roof of St Andrew's Hall. The moment passed and the relationship soured, and was not helped by the untimely death of the town clerk, Arnold Miller, who had done much to bring tolerance and amity to discussions. By the end of the decade the committee had been abolished and the Society had to accept an advisory committee that could make representation to the council's main committees – not quite the same thing as being part of a Council committee.

There was to be one more significant success for the Society in this period. In 1928, for the first time, the Society was able to point to a substantial property, the Strangers' Club in Elm Hill, which would almost certainly have been lost without its intervention. The larger Elm Hill fight was to continue for some time, but this and other successes were wonderful encouragement to a young and still small society.

ERNEST ALFRED KENT (1865–1951)

(Norfolk & Norwich Archaeological Society)

E.A. Kent was an antiquarian and author of distinction who served the Norwich Society from its inception until after the Second World War. He was educated at the old Commercial School, Norwich, and took his Bachelor of Arts degree at Owen's College, Manchester. He seems quite naturally to have succeeded his father in the solicitor's office at Garsett House, St Andrew's Plain. Overlooking the Plain, the old preaching yard of the Dominican Friars, this was a venerable place and, with the passage of years, both Kent and his office acquired the same quality. In 1931 he was elected Fellow of the Society of Antiquaries. At his death the *Eastern Evening News* said that his office contained nearly as many antiquarian works as books of law and that it was doubtful 'whether any man . . . had a wider knowledge than he of the history and antiquities of Norfolk in general and Norwich in particular'. The paper described him as kindly, courteous and often witty, but likely to become very angry when any old and beautiful part of Norwich was needlessly defaced, and said, 'Unfortunately, he saw a good deal of this in his long lifetime, and he never ceased to protest against it.'

The *Eastern Daily Press* was equally laudatory at his death, saying that there was 'not a street – and scarcely a building – within the circuit of the old walls of Norwich whose history he did not know' but that he 'bore his learning modestly and shared it generously'. His contribution to the Norwich Society, both in terms of his knowledge of the city and his good administration over many years, was immense. Kent's office must have seen some lively Society meetings, and he and his brother-in-law, Ralph Mottram, would have been a formidable pair. Kent's writings included a monograph on the Guildhall, and he was co-author with Basil Cozens-Hardy of *The Mayors of Norwich*. The work of the Norfolk and Norwich Archaeological Society was also important to him, and from time to time he contributed to the *Norfolk and Norwich Archaeological Journal* – and to the *Eastern Daily Press* under the pen name *Othinel*. For a time he was president of the Norfolk and Norwich Library and he was one of those who welcomed Queen Mary to the cathedral in 1938, when she reopened the cloisters.

Among so many other things, Ernest Alfred Kent strove to conserve the beautiful church of St Peter Hungate as an ecclesiastical museum and would surely have been very sad to see that its use came to an end in recent times. He was a man of great knowledge but also of great humanity. Well could it be said of him that he served his beloved Norwich quietly but very faithfully in a score of ways.

The magnificent Erpingham Gate, built in 1420 (as was the cathedral choir stall) by Sir Thomas Erpingham in praise of God after his victorious leadership of the sturdy English bowmen at Agincourt in 1415. It is hard to imagine that until the early works of the Norwich Society it had no preservation order upon it.

Norwich City Guildhall, *c.* 1910. This magnificent building was built in the fifteenth century as th
first administrative centre for the mayors and sheriffs of Norwich after the 1404 charter which ma
the city a county in its own right. Only with the creation of the Norwich Society was it realised th
this building, along with such other notable edifices in the city such as the Erpingham and Ethelbe
Gates, Pull's Ferry, St Andrew's Hall and Bishop Bridge, had no preservation order on them.

Bishop Bridge, 1993. Undoubtedly one of the oldest extant water crossings in England, the bridge as we know it today was built by Richard Spynk as part of the city defences between 1337 and 1341. In 1923 the city wanted to widen this ancient bridge. Remedial work had already begun but luckily the Norwich Society was formed just in time to save it. Today the bridge's future has been made all the more secure as its use has been restricted to pedestrians and cyclists. *(Sarah Cocke)*

Whitefriars' Bridge, 1886. A river crossing has been situated here since at least the twelfth century. It takes its name from the Carmelite White Friars who came to Norwich in 1256 and built their extensive priory nearby. The bridge photographed here dates back to shortly after Kett's Rebellion, when the earl of Warwick ordered the destruction of the previous bridge to keep the rebels out. Sadly, this bridge lost its own battle for survival in 1924 when it was taken down under a widening scheme. It was also the first battle lost by the Norwich Society; but, as a compromise, the stones of the bridge were carefully taken down and numbered with a view to re-erect at another site at a later date. Unfortunately the stones have mysteriously disappeared – it is said they were used in error as hard core rubble during postwar reconstruction work on Aylsham Road!

astle Meadow, 1926. Once a
uiet crescent of solicitors and
otaries, Castle Meadow
ecame a bustling thoroughfare
ith the coming of the trams in
900. By the 1920s the
mount of traffic was such that
widening scheme was enacted
d it was suggested that the
ew county police station
ould be constructed near the
irehall, which would have
eant extensive destruction of
e castle gardens and
sruption to part of the castle
ound itself.

ford Place, c. 1926, viewed with our backs to Skipper's Anchor buildings and the frontage of Curl
others on the left, which mirrored the design of the Anchor buildings. Orford Place triangulated around
e tram terminus with Burlington buildings, seen to the right of the photograph. With the demise of the
ams in the mid-1930s, enemy action in the Second World War, which saw the destruction of Curl's and
bsequent rebuilding and road development, Orford Place is now far removed from the dreams of its early
entieth-century architects.

Bank Plain, *c.* 1926. Pictured shortly before their demolition in 1926, these are the late Georgian Bank
Buildings including Bartlett Gurney's Bank House, which once rounded the corner of Bank Plain on
Castle Meadow and Agricultural Hall Plain.

Dating from 1993, this view shows the magnificent buildings designed by Norwich architect Edward Boardman
and completed in 1929 for Barclays Bank. A visit to this neo-Georgian edifice with its lofty interior and smart
decor was certainly an experience for any country farmer after a successful day at the cattle market! Times
change and banks apparently no longer seek such significant portals of exchange to court custom in provincial
areas. This wonderful building has recently been sold and is destined for a non-banking future. *(Sarah Cocke)*

admittedly tired-looking Elm Hill viewed from the Wensum Street end, *c.* 1925. During the nineteenth ntury the yards and houses on the hill had become cramped tenements with families living poor lives in ualid sanitary conditions. To the left can just be seen the gateways to the church of SS Simon and Jude, lose tower collapsed in 1913. The houses in its churchyard had been cleared away some time before and : ancient houses on the nearby Paston Place at the rear of the Augustine Steward House were demolished 1927 under the city works slum clearance scheme – Elm Hill was to be next! We have to be very thankful it folks in the Norwich Society realised that if Elm Hill was demolished there would be no timber-framed eets left in the city in any condition. In 1924 the Norwich Society began the fight to preserve Elm Hill, d by the time the vote came in the City Council chamber the pressure had been such that the eservationists carried the day – but only by one vote!

Elm Hill, 1920s. Looking tired, dirty, worn and uncared for, Elm Hill was an ideal candidate for the slum clearances in Norwich in the 1920s and '30s. Luckily the founding fathers of the Norwich Society realised its importance and as it was just about the last cobbled and gabled street left intact in the city they lobbied for its preservation. Now a treasured heritage gem in the city and a must for any visitor, it should not be forgotten that Elm Hill was only saved from demolition by a majority of one vote in the Norwich Council Chamber! *(P. Armes)*

The gabled Pettus House, 41–43 Elm Hill, when occupied by W.H. West, scales-makers, 1922. This is but a fragment of the fifteenth-century home of the Pettus family. The buildin[g] once stretched down the hill to the church of SS Simon and Jude. It is one of the few buildings on the hill which survived the disastrous fire of 1507; most buildings on Elm Hill thus date from the rebuilding up to the 1520s.

No. 34 Elm Hill, *c.* 1922. Sadly, this wonderful Elizabethan building with its Georgian fenestration and doorways is little more than a redundant shop and the location of a sign directing people elsewhere. Within ten years Elm Hill was saved and restoration was under way. Today this wonderful building is the treasured home of a fine art gallery and picture framers. *(P. Armes)*

2

The 1930s

A Forceful Voice in a Changing City

The entrance to Bayfields Yard at the top of Ber Street, opposite the junction with Finkelgate, *c.* 1930. Perhaps outright criticism of those who demolished so much in the early twentieth century can be a little tempered when looking at a photograph like this. Many of the historic buildings we know in the city today have been lovingly restored and any proposal to pull them down would generate widespread outcry. This photograph, however, shows that in the 1920s families were still living in squalor in cramped and run-down old buildings. When money was short in the Depression harsh decisions were made and little time or money could be spared for the preservation of decrepit old buildings. *(P. Armes)*

Arthur Batchelor had been quick to see the amount of work likely to fall upon the secretary of the Society and had been joined, during the previous decade, by a solicitor with antiquarian tastes, Ernest Alfred Kent (1865–1951). These joint secretaries had also fulfilled the treasurer's duties. Kent was to remain active in the Society's affairs until after the Second World War, and became its treasurer. His sister was married to R.H. Mottram, a bank official turned author, a connection which resulted in Mottram's appointment as secretary in succession to Batchelor. Mottram held this position until 1955, and was an eloquent defender of what he believed to be the best of Norwich. He was closely involved with the Society's annual reports, in one of which reference was made to the city walls, which in places were being exposed to view by redevelopment. The piece plainly shows a love of place and of the achievements of an old city, which was at odds with the beginnings of the rush to suburbia: 'What purpose does such a wall serve? It is no longer a means of defence. It does not even mark the limits of the modern city. Yet the wall does serve a purpose in emphasising the privileges and obligations of citizenship. Here was and is wealth and good government to a degree that the open country can never know . . . something kept in common and valued as such.'

In 1930 the Norwich Society opposed the widening of Sir John Soane's Blackfriars Bridge, and the work was not carried out. The next year it mounted a campaign to stop the demolition, in the furtherance of street widening, of the Boar's Head at the junction of Surrey Street with St Stephen's Street. This grand old building survived, but not for long – destroyed by German bombs eleven years later. Another public house was threatened in 1932 when plans for a new City Hall threatened the demolition of the Sir Garnet Wolseley. The Society actively opposed the demolition and the Sir Garnet survived.

A positive move was taken in 1935 with the formation of the Amenities Preservation Society. Percy Jewson, the president of the Norwich Society and later that year Lord Mayor, took the lead, proposing the formation of a public utility company 'to handle property requiring reconditioning and not susceptible of such treatment by the Corporation'. The new body's first success was a row of buildings in Oak Street (which were again improved in 1973 by the Norwich Preservation Trust). Later in the 1930s the Amenities Preservation Society restored Cotman House on St Martin at Palace Plain. The Norwich Society itself was still small: in 1934 it still had only sixty-two members, of whom only four paid more than the minimum subscription of half a crown. On the other hand, Curat House, where many meetings took place, could be hired for three shillings and sixpence.

Perhaps the greatest of the pre-war fights also occurred in 1935. The Norwich High School for Girls was quartered in the Georgian Assembly Rooms in Theatre Street and intended to move to more spacious accommodation on Newmarket Road. To raise money the Girls' Public Day School Trust wanted to have the Theatre Street buildings removed from the Ministry's scheduled list, allowing the buildings to be demolished and the site sold to the highest bidder. Allied to the Norfolk and Norwich Archaeological Society, the Norwich Society fought and won: the Assembly Rooms were not removed from the protected list. Fifteen years later they were still in existence and were made available for the use and enforcement of the citizens by the generosity of H.J. Sexton. The Assembly House, as it is known today, became the regular meeting place and in many ways the home of the Society, and now houses the administrator's office.

In 1937 Elm Hill again became a matter of concern to the Society. Having already saved the north side, the Society became aware of the Corporation's desire to give over the south side to light industry. The president made strong representation to the town clerk against the proposals and, at last, the city began to appreciate the wonderful old street in its midst. Firm about Elm Hill the Society may have been, but it was less decisive when considering the City Hall. After deliberating whether the building should be grey or red-brick in colour, it eventually came to no conclusion, leaving the decision to the architects, who chose neither. Norwich City Hall has always divided opinion and does so to this day. It is unfortunate that Robert Atkinson's 'footprint' for the civic centre has never been completely filled, and that even today stub girders project into the void on the St Giles' end of the building. Even so, over sixty years on, there is much to admire in the building that C.H. James and S. Rowland Pierce created – a splendid clock tower, wonderful bronze doors and a superb council chamber. Much has been made of its similarity to Stockholm City Hall, but George Nobbs, in his 1988 booklet *Norwich City Hall*, reminds us that the only common features are that both buildings are of brick and have a clock tower. The Society may have been wise to keep its ammunition for other targets.

In 1938, under the supervision of Professor E.M. Tristam, who had been involved with the cleaning of the roof bosses in the cathedral cloisters, the Society carried out the cleaning and restoration of the important armorial shields on the exterior of the east wall of St Andrew's Church. These shields had been moved there during the rebuilding of the church in 1506. They may well date from the visit of Richard II and his queen, Anne of Bohemia, in 1383. This is the view of Arnold Kent and Andrew Stephenson in their *Norwich Inheritance*. Another date postulated is the granting of the charter to the city by Henry VI in 1404, which made Norwich a county of itself. The restoration was a pleasing practical contribution, brought about at the instigation of E.A. Kent, who was responsible for raising the funds. The decade had seen the Society participate in the meeting of the British Association in Norwich while strengthening its relations with societies in other cities and towns.

Arthur Batchelor retired from the Society's council, where after ceasing to be secretary he had sat as a representative of the Norfolk and Norwich Archeological Society, at the meeting on 31 May 1939. As the Society received its sixteenth annual report there were hopes of a full-scale survey of Norwich by the Historical Monuments Commission. That meeting had also received good news about the church of St George, Colegate, which had been badly in need of attention. On the following day an editorial in the *Eastern Daily Press* referred to the church's associations with John Crome and reported that the Pilgrims Trust was making an award of £200 to 'a fine Church beneath whose shadow the painter lived and within whose walls he was buried'. The paper spoke of 'A long, patient and often ill-rewarded effort in which the Norwich Society has played its part'. With the onset of war there were more pressing priorities for the city, and for a time the Society was in abeyance.

RALPH HALE MOTTRAM (1883–1971)

R.H. Mottram was a Norwich man born into the world of provincial banking where his father was a manager. For a while Mottram followed his father's occupation, but literary ambitions were always in mind. Between 1914 and 1919 Mottram served as an interpreter with the Norfolk Regiment in France, an experience which was to provide the material for his first success as a novelist. After the war Mottram returned to the bank but in 1924 *The Spanish Farm* was published to critical acclaim, winning the Hawthornden Prize. Two sequels followed, *Sixty-Four Ninety-Four* and the *Crime at Vanderlynden's*. In 1927 all three were gathered together and republished as *The Spanish Farm Trilogy*, later to be filmed as *Roses of Picardy*. In this year, encouraged by his friend John Galsworthy, Mottram forsook the bank and decided to earn his living with his pen.

Mottram's sister was married to the Norwich Society stalwart Ernest Alfred Kent, and it may well have been the effect of this relationship that encouraged Mottram to become the Society's secretary in 1930. For twenty-five years Mottram was a strong-minded (Sir Bernard Feilden who was to succeed him says he was 'like flint') and very articulate spokesman for the Society. His utterances have passed into Norwich legend. If Norwich was to become 'Ugly in the Marsh', it would only be after the perpetrators had endured a fusillade of Mottram *bon mots*. He cared deeply for his city. Much of his writing and his work for the Society walked a common path. His novels, with an autobiographical base involving Easthampton, such as *Our Mr. Dormer* and *Castle Island*, and his efforts on behalf of the real Norwich were both concerned with the change that time brings – but also with the enduring beauty and character of an English county town. Some of Mottram's best and most valued work is non-fictional. *If Stones Could Speak* sees the streets and thoroughfares of Norwich as a family, each member with its own slow growth and personality. *Another Window Seat* begins with Mottram as the returning soldier in 1919 and ends with him as Lord Mayor of Norwich attending the coronation of Queen Elizabeth II in 1953. Another honour that must have pleased him was the honorary degree of Doctor of Letters that the still-young University of East Anglia bestowed upon him in 1966.

Keith Skipper in *Norfolk Connection* writes of Mottram's death in 1971. Eric Fowler ('Jonathan Mardle' of the *Eastern Daily Press*), said of him then, 'Nobody else in this city will ever know or express quite so much as he did about the spirit of the place.'

In due time the Norwich Society erected a memorial to Ralph Mottram at St James's Hill on Mousehold Heath, which explains the panoramic view of the city that lies beneath. Nothing could be more appropriate.

ve: Blackfriars or St George's Bridge,
910. A remarkable survivor, this is truly
most aristocratic bridge in Norwich. Built
1784 to replace the sixteenth-century New
dge, the bridge we see today was designed
no lesser architect than Sir John Soane, the
hitect of the Bank of England. In 1930 the
dge was under threat from the planned
ening of St George's Street. It remains
ay thanks to a successful campaign by
Norwich Society.

within's Alley, 1923. Post-First World War
n clearance was gathering great momentum
he city at this time and this charming little
er of Norwich, just off St Benedicts Street,
due to fall too. The Norwich Society,
ther with the Amenities Preservation
ety (formed in 1935), entered into the first
nany joint ventures to preserve historic
dings in the city and managed to save one
k of three cottages here.

St Swithin's Alley showing the passage th
leads past Hampshire Hog Yard, 1936.
With the help of the Amenities Society,
which facilitates funds for the preservatio
of historic buildings, shortly after this ph
was taken began the restoration of these
cottages which, like others, were left to th
city by Mayor Seaman in 1715 for
apprenticing two boys yearly from certai
parishes.

Below: St Swithin's Alley viewed from the
churchyard of St Swithin (now the Norw
Arts Centre), 1993. The row of three
cottages has been wonderfully preserved
but sadly they stand in some isolation –
rest of the timber-framed buildings were
saved from demolition. The cottages are
surrounded by very unsympathetic mode
developments. *(Sarah Cocke)*

Lady Lane looking towards Bethel Street, 1931. Once a short street which ran between Bethel Street and Theatre Street, Lady Lane had a pub at each end. Seen here on the left is the Old Theatre Tavern, while at the Theatre Street end was the Shakespeare, 'a haunt of the less desirable theatre types'. The most notable structure of this little lane was the Methodist chapel of St Peter, the third and largest purpose-built Methodist chapel in the city, opened in 1824. Extensive demolition of this area was carried out in the 1960s to enable the construction of the new Norwich City Library; Lady Lane was demolished to make way for the car park, and even in death given the ignominy of having its name changed to Esperanto Way.

The Old Boars Head on the corner of Surrey Street and St Stephen's, *c.* 1934. This ancient pub, known
its snug which was packed with farmers on cattle market days, dated back over 500 years. The roa
widening scheme for St Stephen's in 1931 threatened its future, and the Norwich Society mounted
successful campaign to save it. Eleven years later its fate was decided once and for all when incendia
bombs dropped by enemy aircraft razed the old building to a shell of plaster and scorched timbers.

Opposite: St Peter's Street viewed from the rear of the Guildhall towards the church of St Peter Mancro
Most of the buildings on the right, be they old coaching inn, hotel, tavern or business premises, date fr
the eighteenth century. They all fell beneath the demolition mace from the mid-1930s as they made way
the new City Hall.

Timberhill, 1936. This charming street of timber-framed buildings has been a lucky survivor over the yea
It narrowly missed the major destruction of the Ber Street area (now occupied by Bonds) and a subsequ
peace-time fire in factory premises. Enduring a few postwar developments, this street is notable for
regeneration and sensitive redevelopment in conjunction with the Castle Mall in the 1990s.

gon Hall, King Street, 1935.

ow: The restored Dragon Hall on King Street, *5.* Much has been done but the Norfolk and *wich* Heritage Trust has raised funds for more *stantial* work on this splendid building. *rah Cocke)*

Cotman House, 1993. The superb three-storey Georgian property in this photograph is Cotman House,
named after one of the leading Norwich school artists, John Sell Cotman. It was here, early in 1824, that
opened his 'School for Drawing and Painting in Watercolours' with terms of 'one guinea and a half
quarter'. Described in the twentieth century as falling on 'evil days', in 1937 the building was under thr
of being pulled down by the city authorities. The Norwich Society intervened, and in a campaign led
Society stalwart Arnold Kent Cotman House was saved in 1938; it was later restored by the Amer
Preservation Society. *(Sarah Cocke)*

e Sons of Commerce
p at 30 Thorn Lane
en it was kept by
derick Bland, *c.* 1937.
the left of the pub may
seen the entrance to
ns of Commerce Court
d to the right Market
e, which joined King
eet to Ber Street.

adise Place (although some may have questioned how appropriate the name was) stood near the top of
ng Sun Lane. This was a typical example of the cramped housing and living conditions authorities
ght to change during the inter-war years. Areas known to be 'hard-up and down-at-heel' were cleared
families relocated to new housing on council estates like Mile Cross. *(P. Armes)*

Union Street, *c.* 1935. This street lined with turn-of-the-century houses built for workers is typical of 'community' streets in the city during the 1920s and '30s. Corner grocery stores and small clothing and boot/shoe shops provided all the basic needs, and the facilities were completed by public houses and, many such areas, 'tin tabernacle' nonconformist chapels. (*P. Armes*)

Below: An unusual view of Quayside, *c.* 1935. In the background can be seen the New Star Inn with the life buoy and drag station close by. In between is Pigg Lane, where the large gabled and dormered building was then occupied as a Church Army Lodging Hostel; many years earlier this building had been the Municipal School. After a chequered life, during the 1990s the area enjoyed a period of revival and conversion to private housing and apartments.

The Dolphin Motor Garage on Drayton Road, when its proprietor was Donald Utting, *c.* 1930. This wonderful study is completed by the horse-drawn Valori Ices wagon on the left with billposters advertising such delights as Johnnie Walker whisky, Brasso, Guinness and the latest offerings of the Regent Cinema. (*P. Armes*)

Freeman's building near the top of Thorn Lane. Between slum clearance and bomb damage very little of this area remains today. *(P. Armes)*

Ber Street by the top of Mariner's Lane. This shows the typical streetscape of the area between the wars. Very little indication of this remains today. *(P. Armes)*

ove: Chapel Street, adjoining Union Street.
Armes)

ompson's Yard, Fishergate. The buildings on
her side have disappeared, demolished in the
er-war slum clearance along with much of the
t of Fishergate. The thoroughfare itself does,
wever, remain, giving access to Loose's car park.
Armes)

The Waterman pub at 142 King Street, *c.* 1930. Here, in the nineteenth century, according to the antiquarian pub historian Walter Wicks, not only did the publican sell beer but cut hair, and advertised with the alluring couplet, 'Roam not from pole to pole, but step in here; Where nought excels the shaving but the beer.' By the late nineteenth and for the first half of the twentieth century this pub was situated a short distance from the Norwich city morgue and many a coroner's inquest was held here. Jurors only had a short walk to the morgue to inspect bodies, and I am sure the publican was only too pleased to oblige with a stiff drink afterwards. (*P. Armes*)

St Anne's Lane looking along Synagogue Street. At the end of the street (behind the camera) stood th
Synagogue, later destroyed by bombing. *(P. Armes)*

Here is Greyhound
Lane, Ber Street, no
far from its junctior
with Horns Lane, th
side of the street far
more open today.
This is a reminder
that Ber Street had
tall buildings on bo
sides; and a remind
also of the hardness
of life. *(P. Armes)*

3

The 1940s

The Damage of War &
the Hopes for Peace

The rubble of Curl's store on Orford Place after the few walls standing were knocked down in the weeks after the main Baedecker raid in 1942. During the nights of 27/28 and 29/30 April 1942 the hits nearest to the city centre occurred. It has been suggested that the bombers were trying to target the new City Hall, which had been opened by King George VI and Queen Elizabeth in 1938. Missing that target the bombs landed on Rampant Horse Street and St Stephen's, which suffered the brunt of the raid instead.

Sixty years on from the Second World War most of us remain all too ignorant of the extent of the losses caused by the bombing. Between 1940 and 1943 Norwich was raided over forty times, resulting in over 340 deaths and 1,092 injuries. In *Norwich at War* Joan Banger quotes the incredible statistic that no fewer than 30,000 of the city's houses were damaged in some measure, while over 2,000 were destroyed.

Two 'Baedeker' raids (so-called because the Germans targeted Norwich as a city of outstanding historical and architectural importance), on the nights of 27/28 and 29/30 April 1942 killed 231 of the city's people and injured 689. On the first of these nights a formation of about twenty-five German aircraft dropped high-explosive bombs on the city in a raid lasting two hours. The second raid followed the pattern of the first, lasting about an hour and a quarter, and this time with a higher proportion of incendiary bombs dropped. Twelve more raids occurred in the following year. Norwich was resourceful: it carried on, encouraged by a visit from the king, who found a vastly different city to the one in which he had opened the City Hall a few years before. Destroyed department stores opened again within the premises of their competitors, and small shops found other spots in the city and traded anew. Spirits were high but could not mask the great damage done to the fabric of the place. Not only were there great gaps at Orford Place, All Saints Green and St Stephen's Street but there was also a cost to be counted in historic buildings. In the old city the churches of St Benedict, St Julian, St, Michael at Thorn and St Paul were destroyed, as were the parish churches of St Bartholomew, Heigham and St Thomas's, Earlham Road. Other places of worship lost were St Mary's Baptist Church, the Quaker meeting house at the Gildencroft and the Jewish synagogue in Mountergate. The remains of St Benedict's Gate had gone together with most of that end of St Benedict's Street. In a shattered St Stephen's, the bombing had destroyed the thatched Boar's Head Inn that had survived earlier civic attacks.

The Society did not wait for the war to end before resuming its business after a break of over three years. The council of the Society met in the Cosin Room of the Stuart and Suckling Halls and resolved to hold the seventeenth annual meeting on 11 June. There was a quick return to fundamentals: the chamber of commerce was informed that the Society's survey of 1934 was still of value as the City Council was 'against altering the character of Norwich'. In 1944 E.A. Kent, a great servant of the Society, resigned as treasurer and Arnold Kent was elected to take his place. The council of the Society started to meet at the new treasurer's office at 71 The Close.

The debate on the future of the city quickened with a pronouncement by Mr Bulman, chairman of the city's postwar development committee, that 'Norwich must be modernised . . . many of the features of Norwich would be difficult to retain in the face of modern requirements'. He thought St Stephen's Street needed to be three times as wide. In 1945 appeared the *City of Norwich Plan* by James and Pierce, which was applauded by the Society as a bold and brave document. The dissenting document by Horace Rowley, the City Engineer, did not win approval since it seemed to place traffic-engineering considerations above all else, proposing dual carriageways along Gentleman's Walk and Duke Street, with similar destructive proposals for Upper King Street, Tombland and Wensum Street. St Stephen's Street was a different matter. Speaking for the Society, Mottram said that not only should St Stephen's be widened (although retaining the curve and not dead straight) but that it should have been done fifteen years earlier when the Society had asked for it. The congestion of St Stephen's had diverted traffic through Westlegate, All Saints' Green and Surrey Street, which should have been reserved for professional and residential occupation. He said, 'Cinemas and bus stations can always be rebuilt and may be all the better for it.'

Mottram saw traffic as the great danger to the character of the city. The *Eastern Daily Press* took him to task, seeing nothing in the traffic proposals for Norwich likely to do greater damage than that done in the previous twenty years by the 'erection of so many tasteless, incongruous and pretentious buildings' that marred the façade of most important city streets. Arnold Kent and Andrew Stephenson in *Norwich Inheritance* were prescient in seeing the true threat: streets were accretions, with man, time and accident all concerned in their creation. The Norwich Society, with others, was being asked by the city authorities to advise what buildings should be preserved because of their interest. This showed a helpful attitude 'but such hunting of museum pieces does little good, for tampering with these streets, partial widening, partial reconstruction, means their destruction'. Some years were to pass before the truth of these words was recognised.

During 1946 a press editorial paid a pretty compliment to the Society – with perhaps a slight sting in the tail. Praising the achievements of the Society and recognising its importance to the city, it saw it as composed of enlightened and cultured people, but hoped that in time more people would come forward to form a body open to all, including the trades union and manual workers.

In May 1947 the Society joined with the Corporation to fight off a threat from the military who wanted to use 150 acres of Mousehold Heath as a permanent training ground. War and the nearness of two barracks had meant that much training had already taken place there, but the city had retained control of the Heath. The threat of permanence and exclusion of the citizens was another matter. Strong representation averted the threat and this wild and wonderful space, the sometime resort of the writer George Borrow and his Romany friend Jasper Petulengro, remained for all to enjoy.

Consultation with the town planning committee in 1948 delayed the annual meeting until 23 November: held at the Stuart Hall, the meeting stood in memory of Helen Colman, a founder member of the Society, who had died that day. It was noted that the hall had been given to the city by Helen and her sister Ethel. It takes its place with others, such as Strangers Hall and the Lazar House, fine, historic buildings given to Norwich for its citizens to use and enjoy.

The annual meeting for 1949 was held on 5 April. The next day an editorial in the local press commended the Society for taking an interest in 'things less than 150 years old'. The Society had praised the Corporation for good, though insufficiently varied, council houses, the layout of the new council flats in the Union Street area, the restoration of Pull's Ferry and Cambridge House on Tombland and some 'charming cottages in Ber Street'. The press suggested that the Society should consider making awards or giving written certificates where good work had been carried out in the city.

Allowing for the Society's stern comments about some new, 'hideous', gas heaters in St Andrew's Hall, the year and the decade ended quietly. Things were not to remain so for very long.

ARNOLD KENT (1898–1976)

When the Norwich Society resumed its activities in 1943, with the war not yet won, one of the first changes was in the role of treasurer when Arnold Kent succeeded E.A. Kent. Although not related they shared a deep love of their city and a willingness to defend its character. The baton of trusteeship had been passed from one to the other. Arnold was born in 1898 and saw service in the First World War. Returning to the city, he qualified as an accountant in 1921. Except for a spell in London between the wars he was to spend his whole career in Norwich working in the Cathedral Close and remaining an active consultant with his firm. He was very much a man of the city, living in Elm Hill and concerning himself with many aspects of its life. In addition to his work with the Norwich Society – treasurer until 1969 and briefly president until that office was assumed by succeeding Lord Mayors – Kent was also chairman of the Norwich Magistrates in the late 1960s and assistant secretary of the Friends of Norwich Cathedral for over twenty years. In his younger days he had acted with the Norwich Players at the Maddermarket Theatre and was a friend of the Players' founder, Nugent Monck.

For all this, it is as a photographer that Kent will probably be best remembered. He took hundreds of photographs of Norwich over the years and has left a fine legacy. An early book of his work, a collaboration with Andrew Stephenson, is *Norwich Inheritance*, published in 1948, which gives a quite wonderful picture of the city at that time. Kent's photographic record and Stephenson's text caught Norwich in a mood of uncertainty, not unlike the one after the earlier war that had brought the Norwich Society into being, when change threatened the essential quality of the city. They were worried and feared for the future: 'The renaissance of a beautiful city must be strenuously willed and planned and struggled for, since beauty and grace no longer come naturally to our builders and those who plan to build. Today, ostentation has finally ousted urbanity from our towns.' In the year before Kent's death he and his friend Stephenson came together again for an exhibition *Thirty Years On*, recalling the book and making biting criticisms of some modern developments. Other books featuring Arnold Kent's work are *Norwich Churches*, where he collaborated with Noel Spencer, former head of Norwich School of Art, and *Norwich in Pictures*, published in 1971.

On Kent's death the *Eastern Daily Press* said that he could be 'fiercely persistent in his defence of old Norwich'. He was a great servant of the Society and the city itself.

The burnt-out shell of the Midland and Great Northern Railway City station. This gaunt sentinel can only hint at the hell this area suffered on the nights of 27/28 and 29/30 April 1942. The city was attacked with high-explosive and incendiary bombs as part of Hitler's new strategy of trying to destroy historic provincial cities in an attempt to break morale. His information was derived from a popular pre-war guidebook series – so these attacks became known as the 'Baedeker' raids.

Trenches are dug to form public air raid shelters on the cattle market, c. 1939. This area is a historic site, having formed part of the castle bailey. Its excavation in the 1980s was quite probably made possible by the digging of these wartime ditches.

Workmen struggle to repair the damage in a bomb crater on Exchange Street after one of the early raids.

Opposite: Not all fires were caused by enemy action in wartime, and this tragic scene is a case in point. I the early hours of 23 October 1940 a fire was discovered at the Back of the Inns. Four city fire appliances, number of trailer pumps and over 200 firemen took over three hours to get the fire under control. Fire hose stretched as far as Duke's Palace Bridge and London Street, drawing water to the fire. The area affected b fire, smoke and water damage ran from the Castle Hotel to the rear of the Fifty Shilling Tailors on th Haymarket. Towards the Royal Arcade three houses were also burnt out. Businesses always find it hard t recover after fires but with the problems of wartime rationing their recovery was made doubly hard.

Early morning, St Stephen's Street,
28 April 1942. Firemen still struggle to
put out the fires sparked by the rain of
incendiary bombs which fell across the cit
the previous night. In the centre right of
this photo may be seen the burnt out shel
of the Boars Head public house. The rubb
of Curl's Store on Orford Place after the
few walls standing were knocked down in
the weeks after the main Baedeker raid in
1942. During the nights of 27/28 and
29/30 April 1942 the nearest major hits
to the city centre occurred. It has been
suggested the bombers were trying to
target the new City Hall, which had been
opened by King George VI and Queen
Elizabeth in 1938, but the bombs landed
on Rampant Horse Street and St Stephen',
which suffered the brunt of the raid
instead.

This 1942 view of the rubble of Curl's store looks out across Orford Place towards the Bell Hotel an
Burlington buildings, which were lucky to escape the same fate. Blown out glass in the window
surrounding the area is still clearly visible.

The site of Curl's store with the church of St Stephen on the left and Haymarket cinema on the right. The ruins of Curl's store were cleared and a concrete basin was made. It was filled with 270,000 gallons of water to become a static water tank for the use of fire appliances in the event of future raids. Thought to have been one of the largest static water tanks in the country, it was to prove an invaluable asset to fire-fighters in future raids.

Caley's chocolate factory, Chapel Field, 1942. Stark ruins and hideously twisted metal characterise the damage to factories inflicted after the Baedeker raid. In Norwich Caley's were not alone as such familiar industrial landmarks as Coleman's Wincarnis Works, Odol Factory, Twiddy's coach works and Bullard's old Mineral Water Factory all suffered in the same raid.

Another view of Caley's chocolate factory, Chapel Field, 1942. When the raid was over and the smoulderin buildings had been thoroughly dowsed by fire hoses, over many hours local children slipped into the ruin and, carefully avoiding the chunks of melted glass, were able to feast on chunks of melted chocolate – heavily rationed treat in wartime. There is many a full (and upset) tummy recalled after that feast! It worth noting that the rubble from the damaged city made an ample supply of hardcore to the airbases bein constructed around the county. Much of the rubble from Caley's was taken to Tibenham to go under th runway being built there.

The junction of Barn Road, Grapes Hill and St Benedict's, 1942. In the distance the tower of St Giles Church looms in defiance of the devastation below it. The nearer round tower of St Benedict's stands wit quiet dignity as the people who lived around it mourn their losses. This little church had its main bod blown to ruins. Only the tower stands today, a silent reminder of the Baedeker raid.

Pictured shortly after the clearance of this area after the Baedeker raid of 1942, the Roman Catholic church of St John stands firm, but poor old Barn Road and Grapes Hill have little left that is undamaged. At St Benedict's Gates a bomb thought to be not less than 1,000 kg tore the building up from the foundations and gouged a huge crater across the road. Local people really thought 'they've got us this time'.

The damage to Oak Street shortly after the raids of 27/28 and 29/30 April 1942. This is a view well remembered by Andy Anderson who saw the street the afternoon after the raid.

The shell of the Trafford Arms and houses on Grove Road after the air raid of 27 June 1942. This wa
another attack when firebombs rained across the city, extensive damage was incurred and lives were lost.
was also in this raid that the church of St Michael at Thorn was gutted by fire.

The badly burnt shell of part
of the Norfolk and Norwich
Hospital and Nurses Home
shortly after the raid of
27 June 1942. As Joan
Banger points out in *Norwich
at War*, 'The heroines of this
raid must surely have been
the grimy, dishevelled nurses'
who, despite being wet from
fire hoses and the hospital
being ringed by fire, evacuate
the patients from the cellar to
the grounds where
ambulances and coaches
removed them to the safety
of another hospital a few
miles away.

ids did not end in 1942 and attacks on Norwich were carried on until 1943. In one of the last raids, after
rviving a number of minor hits, Harmers' Clothing Factory on St Andrew's Street received a direct hit.
daunted, Harmers carried on their business of making battle dress and wartime clothing in a
efabricated building just outside the city.

Men perched precariously on top of one of the buildings in Orford Place. After the air raids and demolitio
and clearance during the war years, the postwar years would give the city a chance to stand back and
was hoped, carefully consider what to do with what was left.

4

The 1950s

The Society Shows its Teeth

Magdalen Street, *c.* 1959.

In this decade the even tenor of much of the Society's work – its views on the case of the cathedral organ, the rebuilding of St Mary's Baptist Church and what Philip Hepworth has called the 'usual casework' – contrasted vividly with two major events: its legal challenge to the Corporation at the start of the decade and the newly founded Civic Trust's scheme for Magdalen Street towards its end. It is also the time when R.H. Mottram's long service as secretary of the Society came to an end. Mottram was succeeded by an architect, Bernard Feilden, who in a different way was to leave an equal mark on Society affairs.

The legal challenge arose over Tombland, the city's market place in Saxon times, and emphasised the Society's regard for the rights of the citizens. At this time, with changes in local government still in the future, Norwich Corporation consisted of 'The Lord Mayor, Aldermen and Citizens of Norwich' with the City Council as its sole agent. In the Society's view, the Corporation's representation of the citizens did not give it a right to take away their privileges that had existed for centuries. Tombland possessed a few stalls, including a florist and confectioners. They were not permanent structures. In 1951, Festival of Britain year, with Norwich as a main provincial centre for events and expecting a visit from Princess Elizabeth, the Corporation thought it was time to tidy things up. It started to put down brick and concrete foundations for the stalls. The Society objected, regarding Tombland as a fine and beautiful square that had been open to the city's inhabitants since Saxon times. Gaining the support of the Georgian Group and others, the Society approached the Minister for Town and Country Planning, who declined to intervene. The Society then took a step of some boldness: in the name of its treasurer, Arnold Kent, and in spite of what Hepworth has called 'its ever insubstantial funds', it took the Corporation to the High Court where Mr Justice Vaisey found in the Society's favour. The Corporation accepted the decision and made no attempt to reverse it, although there was resentment among some City Council members. The Society, for its part, promptly issued a new recruiting leaflet reminding people of its past successes and its latest good work in preventing encroachment on ancient privileges.

A building that had been saved from demolition in the 1930s, not least by Society endeavours, came into its own early in this decade. The Assembly House, after a history as a College of Secular Canons, a great town house for the Hobarts, the Georgian Assembly Rooms, a Girls' High School and wartime camouflage centre, emerged delightfully as a place of eating, meeting and eminently civilised concourse. The Sexton Arts Trust established it for the use of the citizens of Norwich and it has flourished in that role to this day. It also became very much the home of the Norwich Society, which in time was to move its office here.

Bernard Feilden had first assisted with the duties of secretary when R.H. Mottram had been Lord Mayor in 1953. In 1955 he took over the post from Mottram, who remained on the council of the Society. Mottram had been a fine spokesman for the Society over twenty-five years, leaving no one in doubt as to the Society's stance. Feilden saw early that something was missing – an added legitimacy. A councillor asked him how many people he represented. When he answered giving the quite small membership of the Society, the councillor said. 'I represent 125,000.' The lesson struck home and Feilden started to think of structural changes to the Society and ways of increasing its membership.

In 1957 the Civic Trust proposed to the City Council a joint project which would 'show how the appearance of some given area in the city, could be improved, without major alterations or expense, if all concerned could be persuaded to work together'. Magdalen Street was chosen because its problems were thought to be typical of many other streets in many other areas. It was said that "Magdalen Street is and always has been, the main street of the quarter of Norwich lying 'over the water'." Almost all the property owners in the street cooperated in a scheme concerned with the painting of buildings, the removal of clutter and better signing. The Trust had a charismatic founder and president, who was also a member of the Cabinet, Duncan Sandys, who in May 1959 was to lead a tour of inspection, accompanied by 500 delegates from all over the country. The impact was considerable, and for all too brief a time Magdalen Street was in the minds of many in this country and beyond. It was the first major scheme of the Civic Trust and was to be followed by other schemes in Burslem, Windsor and Haddington. In Windsor the scheme was inaugurated by the queen, who said 'Many cities and towns . . . could benefit from this treatment.' It is understandable that it is the Trust's involvement that is best remembered but it was Bernard Feilden who was appointed to work with the Trust's architect, Misha Black. More local architects known as the 'Magdalen Street Group' worked with Feilden, including Derek Bond, Sheila Gooch, Barry Hastings and a future chairman of the Society, Edward Skipper. Ahead lay nemesis in the form of the traffic engineer and his child, the Magdalen Street flyover, which was to destroy much of what had been achieved. For a while, however, Magdalen Street basked in an unexpected glory.

Other matters engaging the Society's attention during this period were the sites of bombed churches. The tower of St Benedict was saved but the ruins of St Michael at Thorn and St Paul's disappeared with but a tablet to show their former existence. This was also the fate of the Tabernacle, the seat of early Methodism in Norwich. The Society regretted the loss of the remains of St Michael at Thorn. For some years after the war the walls stood picturesquely in Ber Street, with some small thorn trees growing in the Churchyard. As a stabilised ruin and garden, the remains of St Michael could have brought some grace into a busy street. The site is today used for car parking.

The annual meeting of the Society in December 1959 was attended by seventy members, the largest attendance to date. It was decided to have a figurehead president, and when Michael Bulman as Lord Mayor accepted the post, the precedent was established of asking the Lord Mayor annually to undertake the role. The Society's council became a prestigious, titular body, with real responsibility descending upon an executive committee, which was to meet monthly. There is perhaps an echo here of the earliest days of the Society, when a committee was appointed and told to establish priorities. The scene was set for other changes that would unfold in the next decade.

Sir Bernard Feilden, cbe (1919–)

Sir Bernard is inclined to say, 'I came from nowhere', which is another way of saying he had a varied and interesting youth. One of five brothers, his early years were spent in London, Canada and Bedford, the last being his place of residence when war broke out in 1939. A member of the Territorial Army at that time, he says that his four and a half years of war service were an uncomplicated part of his life: 'One did as one was told.' In fact he spent those years in the Indian Army, serving in Persia/Iraq, the Middle East and Italy, and he retains to this day an affection for his regiment, a famous one, and the people of India. With the war over, he completed his training as an architect and married a Norfolk girl – which brought him to Norwich.

In the city he worked for four years with Edward Boardman & Son and then decided to set up on his own. Looking back he says that at that moment he seemed to have no prospects at all. Things brightened substantially with the commission for the Trinity Presbyterian Church, to be built on Unthank Road to replace the previous church destroyed by bombing in Theatre Street. When he was joined by David Mawson, the now renowned firm of Feilden & Mawson was established. Feilden was to make his name as a cathedral surveyor by using quite radical techniques to stabilise the tower and spire of Norwich Cathedral when much established opinion believed they would have to be taken down and rebuilt. Sir Bernard went on to be surveyor to both St Paul's and York Minster as well as Norwich.

It was standing in as Society secretary during R.H. Mottram's lord mayoralty in 1953 that enmeshed him in the work of the Society, but it was Arnold Kent's defence of Tombland that had earlier inspired him to become a member. Kent and Stephenson's *Norwich Inheritance* introduced him to the city's glories. In 1955 he succeeded Mottram as secretary of the Society, with a committee that consisted of Percy Jewson, Arnold Kent, Colonel Glendenning and F.H. Swindells, and set in train changes that were to lead to a greatly increased membership and a paid, part-time secretary/organiser. On his appointment as secretary, Bernard Feilden saw the primary task of the Norwich Society as confronting the problems of 'Town Planning in Norwich'. He saw the members of the Society as essentially preservationist and 'hoped to turn them into conservationists'. He saw the value of bringing in young architects – and others – into the work of the Society, 'Young Turks', brimful of ideas. He liked to keep the membership busy with surveys such as the Society's 'Leisure Survey', which produced the perhaps surprising result that more people were engaged on a Friday evening with some sort of educational activity than were in the pubs or cinemas. Another survey showed that a 'bumbled off' London Street, where maintenance work was being carried out, had not resulted in a loss of trade for the shops. The Society used this to press for permanent pedestrianisation of the street that, once achieved, gave national prominence to London Street and was the forerunner of schemes throughout the country of pedestrian priority in existing streets.

There was nothing of the parochial about Bernard Feilden. He saw the worth of Norwich and wanted the very best for it. He brought high-profile speakers to the city to ensure that the Society's outlook was a broad one. These included Colin Buchanan to speak on traffic matters; he was to present to the Minister of Transport a proposal for 'ring and loop' in Norwich that was published and publicised by the Society.

For a man who on his appointment as secretary regarded himself 'as a most unsuitable person', Bernard Feilden has left a very distinctive mark on the Society. Philip Hepworth's words are still relevant; the Society today runs substantially on the lines Bernard Feilden introduced in 1959.

ıgdalen Street after its regeneration, *c.* 1959. From this angle the basic shape of the buildings and street s changed little; sadly, most of the smartly painted trade signs seen here have now disappeared as sinesses have sold up or moved and premises have changed hands over the years.

The Haymarket and Gentleman's Walk, 1950. In the days after the war when rationing was gradually bei
phased out, the people on the street are still wearing their utility coats and other clothing. Signs
affectionately remembered businesses like Lambert's Mecca, which sold loose teas and coffee, Lipto
Grocers and Backs, once famous for their 'long bar' can all be seen.

The Haymarket and
Gentleman's Walk, 1993.
Now fully pedestrianised, thi
area is filled with foot traffic
by the thousand every day.
Although far removed from
the days of perambulating
dandies from which
Gentleman's Walk takes its
name, it is still a place to me
greet, mardle and be seen.
(Sarah Cocke)

e King's Head pub at 44–48 Magdalen Street, 1959. Basking in the glow of their recent renovation it was
the King's Head that the Rt Hon Duncan Sandys MP, President of the Civic Trust, stopped while on his
it to the city to raise a glass to the success of the project. Beside the pub at nos 44–48 is a superb
imple of a typical eighteenth-century merchant's house and shop. When this photograph was taken the
siness premises were occupied by Smith and Sons, chemists.

ortly after the completed
iovation project the smartly
ainted shop fronts and bright
w blinds and signs show
gdalen Street to be in its
stwar heyday of 1959.
the middle of the picture can
seen the Regency Barclays
nk building and the junction
Magdalen Street and
tolph Street.

The area of Magdalen Street known for generations as Stump Cross, *c.* 1959. Located here was a short row of affectionately remembered shops, Mann's restaurant and the Dolls' Hospital. On the right of the picture the Regency Barclay's Bank building can also be seen. Within a handful of years this bright, restored area of the city was hammered down to make way for the inner link road's concrete flyover.

The demolition of houses on the corner of Queen Street and Tombland, *c*. 1950. This building w
transformed into Woolwich House, the Norwich city office of the Woolwich Equitable Building Socie
Constructed with smart military pargetting and tastefully decorated with bronze plaque castings
nineteenth-century army ordnance, this building was capped off with a weather vane in the shape of
artilleryman and cannon.

The Haymarket, *c*. 1959. Dominating the scene is the old Haymarket cinema with the classic 192
frontage of Burton's outfitters to the left. Both of these buildings were demolished in 1959 to make way
new shop premises.

5

The 1960s

The Years of Change & Growth

London Street, 1967.

Agreat deal happened during this decade, both within the Society and the city. The Society appointed Jean Ogden as its first paid, part-time secretary/organiser, and saw its membership grow to over a thousand. The city, perhaps realising that there were elements of the town planning process that did not necessarily fit easily into the remit of a city engineer, divorced town planning from engineering and established a separate department. Both of these appointments were considerable departures from what had been considered the norm, and both were successful. For its part, the city chose Alfred Wood, a 38-year-old consultant in planning who had experience in both the private and public sectors, as its planning officer, a man who approached his task with zest and who established a department of high quality.

The Society had its successes during the period: the Barking Dicky in Westlegate was not lost to the city, and as a picturesque thatched building survived contained to make a charming contribution to the street, albeit overshadowed by one of Norwich's most unfortunate modern buildings, the Glass Tower. The demolition of Ivory House, built in All Saints' Green as an artillery barracks, was successfully opposed, and a Riverside Walk for the city was promoted. All were important and not least the last, which did much to overcome the long-established habit in Norwich of regarding its river as an industrial conduit or a backyard. Later in the decade came the pedestrianisation of London Street, which played a major role in developing new attitudes to the pedestrianisation of the city centre in Norwich and further afield.

There was one loss that appears to have been so needless that it still angers forty years on. Brian Ayers, in his book *Norwich*, writes of the years after the war, in Norwich and in many other cities, when reconstruction was accompanied by a severe attack upon the historic environment. As a leading archaeologist Ayers obviously writes from that perspective, but in citing the Norwich losses, a long stretch of city wall in Grapes Hill, the site of the Augustinian Friary and the galleried White Swan Inn with its vaulted undercroft, he includes the New Star Inn on Quayside. This gabled building gave beauty and proportion to the Quayside façade and, in Andrew Stephenson's words, 'Overlooked the busy quay in the Tudor prosperity of the woollen trade. The main road from here to the market-place was by Elm Hill, St Andrew's and Dove Street.' Ayers tells of the story, which he says may be apocryphal but has the ring of truth, that when the Inn was condemned to demolition in 1963 a councillor spoke of it being the resort of prostitutes 'we don't want that sort of thing, do we?' How easily and how foolishly we destroy our links with the past!

Much less depressing was the establishment of the Norwich Preservation Trust, a partnership between the City Council and the Society. The aim of the Trust was to acquire and renovate old properties in the city and bring them into everyday use. This body took over the activities and assets of the old Amenities Preservation Society and became one of the most successful building preservation trusts in England. Some buildings were sold on to fund future projects and some were retained on a rental basis. The Trust regarded itself, and still does, as 'the bank of last resort' and only stepped in when no other initiative was forthcoming. There are buildings dotted all over the city, often rescued from complete dereliction, that may well have been lost had the Trust not existed.

Traffic and its effects remained a constant theme in Society affairs throughout the 1960s. Jean Ogden's appointment was discussed in January 1965 in the regular *Eastern Evening News* feature, 'Over the Tea Table' by Whiffler. On the same page was a photograph of a model of the projected Magdalen Street flyover. This was the subject of a fierce and prolonged argument between the modernists, those believing that Norwich had to be changed drastically if it was to continue to thrive, and those, with the Norwich Society very much in the van, who found its positioning essentially destructive. The Society favoured a route aligned with the edge of the old city. In March of the same year W.K. Smigielski, Leicester's Polish-born planning officer, addressed the Society on traffic matters. He received what the press described as 'an almost rapturous reception'. He spoke of the likely tyranny of the motor car and its effect on a sophisticated, rich and varied urban civilisation. His remedies included interchange car parks, integrated transport plans and monorails. The City Council's thinking changed at this time, with an abandonment of wide through roads in favour of something remarkably akin to the proposals of Colin Buchanan, effectively 'ring and loop'. The Magdalen Street controversy reached the *Manchester Guardian*, which mentioned the charm of the city but spoke of its urban population being likely to increase from 160,000 to 350,000 by the year 2000. Those, however, were the days when 'city regions' were still within the realms of possibility. Could such days come again?

The multitude of parish churches in Norwich, many left with small congregations after their resident populations had been diminished by clearance orders between the wars, were both a glory and a worry. Dr Launcelot Fleming, the bishop of Norwich appointed a Commission under the chairmanship of Lord Brooke, the former Home secretary Henry Brooke, to consider what should be done with these churches of the inner city. In August 1968 the Norwich Society presented a report to the Commission. The press said 'this seems to have failed to attract appreciable support'. The Society had suggested alternative uses for some of the churches and, whatever the initial reaction, this was what eventually happened. The City Council purchased the freehold of a considerable number of the churches that were made redundant and the Norwich Historic Churches Trust came into being to administer them. The scheme has had its critics, notably Simon Jenkins in recent times, but nowhere in England did a city have such a number of buildings with which to deal. The solution was a brave one, which inspired other places and which saved many buildings of great importance to the Norwich scene.

Towards the end of the decade conservation areas came into being with the advent of the Civic Amenities Act of 1967, and the Society made its recommendations. There was one item of controversy with a proposal for a nine-storey tower at the Maid's Head Hotel. This was accepted by the City Planning Committee, with the Chairman saying it had become a principle of planning to make the skyline as interesting as possible, and dismissing a press photographic impression of how the 'modern perpendicular' tower would look from Tombland as 'phoney'. The press was full of critical letters but the scheme had received approval. Its non-implementation was a great relief to many.

Jean Ogden (1923–2000)

In what may be termed the 'modern' history of the Norwich Society, Jean Ogden played a most important part. It was her hard work and organisational powers that built up a large Society. Bernard Feilden was the man who realised, after an encounter with a city councillor, that size meant legitimacy, but it was Jean Ogden who went out and found the people to produce it.

Jean was very much of the city of Norwich and the city was important to her throughout her life. Born Jean Gunn, from her father's side of the family she inherited an interest in the city: one uncle was much concerned with the design of the Norwich Gates at Sandringham House; another uncle was a taxidermist with a shop on All Saints' Green. On her mother's side the connections were military, warrant officers and non-commissioned officers in the Royal Artillery. This connection was to continue when she married John Ogden, a former commissioned officer in the Royal Horse Artillery who was an enormous help to Jean during all her time as secretary/organiser of the Norwich Society. After her education at the Norwich High School for Girls, Jean worked for a short time at the Midland Bank, but the advent of the Second World War changed the course of her life. Serving as a commissioned officer in the Auxiliary Territorial Service gave scope for her natural organisational skills. Later those same skills were to be put to good purpose in the service of the Norwich Society.

Important as her success was in building up the membership of the Society from about 300 in 1964 to 1,500 or so at its peak, Jean Ogden was very much more to the Society than this. She was always ready to 'charge the guns' in the interests of the Society. At a time when the Society had conducted a survey, at the request of the City Council, of buildings for consideration of 'listing', Jean learned that a firm wished to expand by demolishing a block of buildings enclosed by Westlegate and Timberhill. Indeed, the Society was due to hold a public meeting to discuss the scheme. Jean telephoned the Department of the Environment to find out which buildings were to be listed, and that department telephoned the City Council to find out what the Norwich Society was. As Jean was about to leave for the meeting the department telephoned to say that seventeen buildings were to be listed in the Timberhill/Westlegate area. The meeting was cancelled and the scheme was rejected.

There were other interests: Jean was a founder member of the Eaton Townswomen's Guild and she helped to bring the prestigious Norwich Ladies' Luncheon Club into being. She was a magistrate on the Norwich Bench for many years. Jean was also an amateur actress of quality and a great fundraiser for the Society. Strong-minded and forthright, she was capable of ruffling a few feathers along the way, although most of the feathers were soon smoothed. Jean was a key player at a most important time in the development of the Society.

Above: Gabled houses on the corner of Palace Street and St Martin at Palace Plain, *c.* 1965. Such houses, many of them of Tudor origin with later additions, were to be found in appalling states of repair across the city well into the twentieth century. Many such buildings were torn down in the slum clearances of the turn of the century and 1930s, but those which survived the purges have, in the main, gradually been restored. These houses on the corner of Palace Plain have been restored, along with the careful restoration of the historic buildings in the area, to make Palace Plain one of the best extant example of a Norwich 'Plain'.

The New Star Inn on Quayside, *c.* 1950. After the devastation of the blitz and the work of various societies to preserve the historic buildings of Norwich past, it seems almost incredible that during the reconstruction work of the 1960s more buildings should fall beneath the demolition mace. One such casualty was the New Star Inn. A building of Tudor origin, it was apparently demolished on the grounds of its clientele rather than its state of repair or historical significance.

Looking very smart in its new livery, this is the Norvic Cinema on Prince of Wales Road, *c.* 1960. Dating back to 1912 when it opened as the Norwich Electric Cinema, this picture house was renamed the Norvic in 1949. Lasting just twelve more years, most of this grand old cinema was demolished in 1961. *(P. Armes)*

London Street, 1967.
This unusual view shows
a bustling London Street
complete with road and
two-way traffic.
As demands of the
street grew far beyond
its capacity it was a
close-run race between
partial demolition
and road widening
versus complete
pedestrianisation.

St Peter's Street, 1962. To the left of the base of the mighty tower of St Peter Mancroft Church are the las vestiges of St Peter's Street. The majority of this little street, which ran from Theatre Street to the rear of th Guildhall, was demolished to make way for the new Norwich City Hall in the '30s. Shortly after this photograp was taken these last few Georgian houses were demolished to make way for the new Norwich City Library.

The same view in 1993, with the remains of St Peter's Street or the little lanes in this area which ran up to Lady Lane. Even the last remnants of historic Swan Inn, where Parson Woodforde dined, prize fighters fought and entertainments were enjoyed in its eighteenth-century theatre, were lost for ever as its vaulted cellars were filled in to allow the road to be raised. Today this view has changed again. The car park and the library it served have gone following a disastrous fire in which the library was gutted. This area is now part of the open space known as Millennium Plain in front of the Forum, which contains the new library. (Sarah Cocke)

he junction of Brigg Street and The Haymarket, *c.* 1965.

superb panorama of Norwich City Hall, St Peter Mancroft Church and Market Place, *c.* 1969.

Haymarket, looking towards Brigg Street, *c.* 1965. On the left and right are the old frontages of Internation
Stores and Burtons, but centre stage is the new block of buildings erected after the demolition of the bom
damaged Curl's store and adjoining shops.

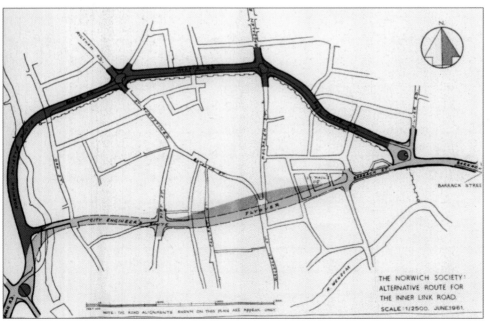

The alternative
plan, suggested
by the Norwich
Society for the
route of the
inner ring road
1961. (*R. Fiske*

6

The 1970s

An Important Birthday & Some Practical Achievements

Get your back into it! Volunteers clear the waste ground behind Elm Hill to create the Oasis in 1975. Wheeling the barrow is Bruce Adam, now a vice-president of the Society.

In his Chairman's Report for 1970 Tony Cartwright said: 'We feel that Norwich is (and always should be) a human city, with a human scale and human values. . . . If by narrowly preserving its buildings, we make a dead museum piece of a city – we fail. But if by sensitively caring for its past and imaginatively creating new possibilities for its future we enrich its life, then Norwich is a better place.' Nearing the end of its fifth decade, the Society was confident in its objectives, seeking to preserve the city's treasures but also making a city for people. Cartwright's words were in many ways an echo of those who had founded the Society. Early in the decade, the city and the Society had to come to terms with a new reality: the old Corporation with all its great powers, and the body with which the Society had dealt since 1923, had slipped away. Eric Fowler's wonderful description of Norwich as 'having, on its better days, something of the feel of a burgher republic' had lost much of its meaning. When the dust settled, Norwich retained its development control responsibility, but the Society had henceforth to think of 'the county' as well as 'the city'.

In 1973 the Society celebrated its Golden Jubilee: there was an exhibition at the City Library, *Fifty and Fighting*, and the Society was honoured by a peal of bells at St Peter Mancroft. The Golden Jubilee edition of the annual report gave a portrait of the city: 'Norwich – cathedral city and market town, centre of manufacturers since the fifteenth century, a city of wealth and prosperity with a fine cultural tradition, and since 1963 home of the University of East Anglia'. The Society was forward-looking: Edward Skipper reported that the Society would continue with its efforts to persuade the government to expedite the construction of the Southern Bypass or Distributor, and Tony Ede, then chairman of the Conservation Group reported on their appraisal of the castle bailey. The report spoke of the castle as a 'supreme jewel in the heritage of Norwich' and the importance of its setting. It was envisaged that underground car parking should be incorporated in to any plans for the old cattle market, '. . . clearly the area must not remain a desert of tarmac and parked cars'.

The new city skyline did not please everyone. Eric Fowler gave a talk at the Assembly House entitled 'Whatever is happening to Norwich?' Among his targets were the wards and maternity blocks at the Norfolk and Norwich Hospital. Time is about to have its revenge upon these buildings, scheduled for demolition after the removal of the hospital to the outskirts of the city. More acceptable contributors to the Norwich scene were its host of medieval churches. The launch of 'The Friends of Norwich Churches' took place at a crowded meeting at the Assembly House with Sir John Betjeman as guest speaker; and the Advisory Board for Redundant Churches, including the very distinguished persons of the Lords Fletcher and Esher and Sir Nicholaus Pevsner, visited the city.

It was a time of exhibitions. The City Council had chosen the restoration of the Colegate area as its contribution towards Architectural Heritage Year in 1975, and the Society organised an exhibition in the church of St George, Colegate, opened by Lady Dartmouth. The area was later visited by the Duke of Edinburgh who was brought upstream in a steam launch, making one of the more picturesque royal visits to the old city.

This area of the city received considerable attention from the Society in these years. 'Operation Oasis' under the leadership of Tony Ede, and with the cooperation of the City Council, transformed a piece of ground at the Fye Bridge end of Fishergate into a semi-wild natural garden. Old Nissen huts were removed and forty volunteers of all ages, including members of YMCA youth clubs, attacked a daunting task with great cheerfulness. Pleasant deeds were also done at Colegate's two great Dissenting churches. Thomas Ivory's Octagon Chapel had originally been surmounted by a wrought-iron finial, that had lasted about one hundred years after its erection in 1756. An exact replica was made by Eric Stevenson of Wroxham and put in place. At the Old Meeting House unsightly wire fencing acting as a boundary to the burial ground was replaced by new wrought-iron railings.

In 1976 the Society put on another exhibition, this time in the church of St Michael at Plea at the instigation of Peter Salt, at twenty-nine years old the youngest member of the executive committee. This was an attempt by the Society to find out what the people of Norwich thought of and wanted for their city. It was called 'Ideas for Norwich' and had been suggested to Peter Salt by what he had seen happening in Bristol.

In 1978, the Society became concerned over changes to Mousehold Heath, which it had sought to protect against military incursions in the 1940s. Now the threat was from natural change: as the amount of open heathland receded, trees, gorse and bracken increased. Also in this year the Society campaigned for the repeal of the law excepting the Church of England from listed building control. The catalyst for this was the demolition of St Phillip's Church in Heigham Road. It had been built in 1871 to serve a population expanding beyond the city walls. Giving his report to the annual meeting, Society chairman Bruce Adam described the loss as the biggest single disappointment of 1977. Earlier there had been another losing battle when the Society had tried to save Spurrell's Lodge, a listed Victorian house within the grounds of the Great Hospital.

Battles over traffic continued. Having seen the 'ring and loop' system replace the threat of wide roads being driven through the city centre, the new concern was that damage would be done by a desire to widen the 'loops'. Duke Street had been widened on the eastern side from its new bridge to the junction with Colegate. The buildings demolished included the Moon and Stars pub. The next phase was the intention to continue the widening, on the same side of the street, from Colegate to Muspole Street, which would have entailed demolishing the corner building at Colegate, the Golden Star pub. This proposal was opposed by the Society as the unnecessary destruction of a pleasant building that had a useful role to play – and which remains a 'pub' to this day. Yet another exhibition was mounted to demonstrate the Society's opposition to the widening of Little Bethel Street and suggested changes to the traffic pattern that would render widening unnecessary. The Society remembered an older method of transportation at Petch's Corner, where a memorial to the Norfolk Wherry was constructed by volunteer labour, appropriately near to the site of an old wherry-building yard.

Away from the city centre, there was the prospect of Newmarket Road being dualled from Cringleford to Daniels Road. The most gracious of the entrances to the city, a greatly changed Newmarket Road would have been hard to bear, and the Society was firm in its opposition to the proposals. Twenty years on, with new trees established to replace those lost by disease, Newmarket Road retains its charm. This was a period of solid achievement for the Society, which had reached a significant anniversary and was an established and respected player on the Norwich scene.

TONY EDE (1927–80)

Tony Ede was one of that not inconsiderable number of gifted people who have come to Norwich from elsewhere and realised quickly they loved the place. He came from Calne in Wiltshire by way of Cambridge University to take up a post in the shoe industry with Sexton, Sons & Everard, and later worked for F.W. Harmer, the clothing manufacturers. One of a group of young, professional men active in the Society and the city, Tony Ede was the type of man who wanted to express his commitment in practical ways. His interests were wide – an exhibition on skate-boarding vying with an amazing capacity for fund-raising in connection with the conversion of the redundant church of St James to a puppet theatre. It is said that Ede raised half a million pounds for this and a similar value in kind, a quite astonishing achievement at any time and particularly twenty-five years ago. At his death, it was discovered he was involved in nearly twenty youth groups, a good illustration of how much he cared for people.

He was also a champion of the city's streets and buildings, a survey of the castle bailey was led by him, and he inspired improvements in the Colegate area at the time of the Heritage Over The Wensum project. Ede had an eye for detail: an exact replacement finial for the Octagon Chapel and good wrought-iron railings for the Old Meeting House burial ground were typical of his enthusiasms. Perhaps the best example of his capacity for 'doing' is the Oasis, an area of land at the junction of Fishergate with Fye Bridge Street, where he led the clearing and planting, leading to real environmental improvement. Here it was Ede's powers of persuasion, in obtaining agreement and cooperation from the City Council, and management that played a vital part. Working with scholars from the Blyth-Jex School, Tony Ede was in his element, a love of city and people coming together in a characteristic way. He was also concerned with Petch's Corner, Jubilee Heights, and the struggle to save Mousehold House. He was an early director of the Norwich Preservation Trust. In working with young people, he found a willing collaborator in Valerie Glauert, the headmistress of the Blyth/Jex School, who was amazed at the effect Ede's leadership had on some of her more difficult pupils. Mrs Glauert tells of Ede finding the splendid trade sign of a stag that had adorned Darlow's the Gunsmith in Timberhill and been removed after a fire, languishing in a builder's yard. Not only did he initiate the stag's return to the shop but arranged for the fire service to hoist it back into its former lofty position. Ede was the very antithesis of those who could not be bothered if the task appeared difficult. He cared and he got things done.

He died all too soon, but he left behind enduring memories of an outstanding Society chairman. It is entirely pleasing that his widow, Janet, is a member of the executive committee in 2003.

London Street, *c.* 1971. The buildings of London Street, some Regency, some from the mid-nineteenth century widening and redevelopment, won the day after Norwich Society intervention on the London Street debate. By the early 1970s a number of pedestrianisation experiments had taken place in the city in areas like Gentleman's Walk, White Lion Street and London Street, all of which are now repaved and used, almost exclusively, by foot traffic.

Hay Hill pictured in the late 1960s. This area was once a market trading area for hay and fodder. By t
end of the nineteenth century it was occupied by a number of pubs. On the left can be seen the survivor, t
St George & Dragon; next door but one was the Golden Pipe and right in the centre, where the statue
seen, was the White Horse. At the turn of the century this area was cleared as part of slum removal a
installation of the new tram network. Where the old White Horse stood a park was set up and opened
1905 with a statue in honour of Norwich's philosopher-physician, Sir Thomas Browne. Since this photo w
taken the old brick Lamberts building behind the statue has been demolished to make way for a mode
clothes shop and the little park cleared away to make way for concrete slabs. Apart from St Peter Mancr
Church and the statue just about everything else seen here has changed – I wonder what Sir Thomas wou
make of it all!

RH Prince Philip, accompanied by Norwich Society Secretary Jean Ogden, greets some of the volunteers
ho made the Oasis possible, when he opened the site on 1 July 1975.

he Oasis, viewed
om the river in
993. The Oasis was a
ece of overgrown
asteland by the
idge between
shergate and the
ver. Cleared by a
am of volunteers
nder the guidance of
e Norwich Society,
is area became a
uite place for public
njoyment and formed
rt of Norwich's
ward-winning entry
r Architectural
eritage Year.
arah Cocke)

Petch's Corner. From the mid-1960s the Norwich
Society actively promoted riverside walks. In 197
they saw the opening of the Oasis followed by
more volunteer labour action here at Petch's
Corner in 1977. In this initiative an area was
cleared and an old wherry mast erected as a
memorial to Norfolk wherries. Constructed near
an old wherry-building yard and with the ancien
Cow Tower as its backdrop, it is still a fine place
stroll through on a sunny day. (*Sarah Cocke*)

Below: The Golden Star on the corner of Colegate
and Duke Street. In the 1970s Duke Street was
undergoing a road-widening scheme. Buildings
already destroyed included the Moon and Stars
public house, and with the proposed continued
widening the Golden Star would have suffered th
same fate. The Norwich Society stepped in and
opposed the unnecessary destruction of this fine
old pub. It is still serving today – Cheers!
(*Sarah Cocke*)

ke's Palace Bridge, Duke Street, 1938. Built to enable the smooth running of the new road over the river
m Maddermarket to Colegate constructed in 1821/2, this was the last bridge to be built across the
ensum within the city walls. In 1855 the city purchased the bridge for a cost of £4,000 and so it
mained until 1972 when a road-widening scheme necessitated the demolition of the old bridge. The
uncil decided to sell the cast-iron arches for scrap, but luckily the Norwich Society stepped in, bought
em and put them into storage.

Carefully does it! When the old Duke Street Bridge was bought by the Norwich Society in 1972 it had to removed to storage, where it remained for another twenty years.

Above: The entrance to Castle Mall car park, Rose Avenue, 1993. After many years in storage the fate of the bridge arches was to be a far happier one than that of Whitefriars' Bridge in the 1920s. They were given to the Castle Mall development, which took the best parts of each arch and had them fully restored and mounted above the car park entrance on Rose Avenue in 1992. *(Sarah Cocke)*

View of the site of the collapsed Corner Café at the St Michael at Coslany end of Colegate, *c.* 1970. To right may be seen the tall gables of Queen Anne House with its distinctive Norwich dormer windows 'lucams', while to the left are some of the sixteenth- and seventeenth-century houses of St Miles's Al Sadly, the new building erected on the site of the old café (which had been housed in a Georgian buildi was, architecturally speaking, not as sympathetic as some would have wished. *(P. Armes)*

7

The 1980s

Public Houses, Superstores & the Castle Mall

The construction of Castle Mall.

This was a period when planning and development matters loomed large. Government planning guidance for local authorities entered a more relaxed phase – too relaxed in the Society's view, where the emphasis appeared to be on competition in retail matters rather than on protection of existing provision, such as Norwich city centre. Applications for out-of-town superstores came thick and fast and the Society fought hard against what it considered to be an excessive threat to the established facilities inside the city walls. At times the city seemed to be a tightly drawn laager, with the 'enemy' camping in increasing numbers just outside. The Society was fortunate in having members willing and able to represent it at public inquiries but there were limits to its resources. In 1983 a Society deputation went to London to see Neil Mcfarlane, a junior minister at the Department of the Environment, where the deputation put its case against repeated applications by firms of supermarket chains and constant planning appeals against refusals. The Society felt that the developers were using the planning system in such a manner to cause '. . . financial exhaustion and collapse . . . on the part of those, including civic societies, opposed to their plans'. The Society's suggested solution was to make the 'wearing down' process more difficult, with financial penalties for unsuccessful developers. It was a difficult time but it had its rewards, and gradually the pendulum swung back towards town centres, although not in time to save some from having their vitality drained by massive out-of-town schemes.

In Norwich it was the need to redevelop the Timberhill area and to consider the future of the old cattle market that was to engage the Society's attention. Timberhill had been ravaged by wartime bombing and the cattle market had been moved to Harford on the city's outskirts. There was an opportunity for the city's central areas to be enhanced – and the city could hardly complain about outside developments if it did not keep its own centre vital and exciting – but the arguments were fierce and prolonged. There were several schemes, each of which had something in its favour. Eventually common features emerged, a rebuilding of the area between Timberhill and Farmers' Avenue and a Mall with car parking *underneath* the old cattle market.

Some people were against the whole idea, as not being the sort of development that married well with the winding streets of the old city. Others disliked the contour of the market being changed, and others still doubted whether such an ambitious scheme could ever be carried through successfully. But there were those who noted that coach loads of people from the city were travelling to Cambridge and Peterborough to use new, large shopping centres. Was Norwich being left behind?

The cattle market area was part of the castle bailey that had been the subject of Tony Ede's report in the 1970s. An ancient monument, its excavation was probably only permissible because of the digging of underground air-raid shelters during the war. The Society had given its support to the scheme but its patience was wearing thin as the decade progressed and little appeared to be happening. It caused a considerable stir by transferring its support from the Estates and General plan to that of the Prudential. The managing director of Estates and General was enraged and said the idea their scheme was taking too long to be '. . . utter rubbish . . .' The city planning officer pointed out that it was entirely possible that both schemes would receive planning permission but the City Council, as landlords, viewed the Estates and General scheme as more commercially viable. As neither scheme could go forward without the consent of the landlords, that was very much that.

Far less contentious was the Society's Diamond Jubilee, celebrated in a most worthy fashion by a service at the cathedral and a royal visit by Princess Alexandra. To mark the sixty years a splendid seat was installed in Elm Hill, designed by Alan Sewell and built by John Barnard. There was a last-minute crisis when the detail on the brass plate was found to be incorrect, but all was well in the end. The *Eastern Evening News* paid a compliment, saying the Society '. . . can take a fair share of the credit for helping to ensure that the fleeting changes of the last six decades have not crushed the life out of the historic environment'. The press could censure as well as praise, and had done so earlier in the decade when the Society had misjudged badly the public mood over a traffic matter. It was not without irony that Elm Hill should be involved, the street that had been the subject of some of the Society's early struggles. The Society had planned a campaign to impose a traffic ban in the historic street but had not anticipated the fierce opposition that came from some traders and residents. Bending before the storm, the Society postponed the campaign.

The city itself was changing in a way that few would have considered possible a decade or two before. Norwich, like England as a whole, was slipping into the post-industrial age. The city had been a place of manufacturing for a very long time, and since the Industrial Revolution that had changed the face of England, a city of shoe factories, food production, brewing and engineering. It was also the home of a great insurance firm that had been founded in the city. To people's surprise, many of the main players were leaving the scene and those that remained were, in the jargon of the times, 'downsizing'. The change was perhaps most marked in shoe manufacturing and brewing. The shoe factories with household names disappeared, the Norvic Shoe Company, Sexton, Sons and Everard, and the rest were lost to the city scene. Whereas at the end of the Second World War Norwich had possessed thirty shoe factories, by the end of the eighties a mere handful survived. In brewing the 'wipe-out' was even more complete: the four main firms, Bullards, Morgans, Steward and Pattesons and Youngs, Crawshay and Youngs, after a series of mergers, coalesced into one concern that was bought by Manns, the London brewer. For a while that firm continued to brew in Norwich, but eventually it too gave up and a long Norwich tradition was effectively over.

As far as 'downsizing' was concerned, nothing illustrated this better than Laurence, Scott and Electromotors, a firm of electrical engineers of the very first rank. Manufacturers of electric motors and switch-gear, the company had made the winch-gear for the great Cunard shipping line and had held important Admiralty contracts during the war. Young soldiers from Norwich on troopships had had their homesickness made worse when able to touch the firm's plate on the various winches on deck. Employing about 3,000 people at the end of the war, the firm's complement was by this time measured in hundreds. Colmans, another labour-intensive employer, became very much smaller. Somehow the service industries and the city's lively retail trade held the ring. There was also a new awareness of the city's history and its architectural and cultural heritage. From being the preserve of people who, in valuing what the past had given to the city were sometimes seen as a barrier to progress, the historic city started to appear as eminently desirable and perhaps even a contributor to economic prosperity in the future. The Society watched the changing scene rather anxiously.

From being in the van in pedestrianisation with London Street, the city had become rather complacent and had dropped behind other centres. There was a determined attempt to catch up and increase the number of pedestrianised streets in the central area. The most contentious area was Gentleman's Walk and the Haymarket. In many ways this was the most appropriate place imaginable. In those far off days when the gentry had been impressed by the large market and the craftsmen surrounding it, the area in front of the market had been kept free of stalls and swept regularly to allow the people of quality to promenade more easily. Now, in more democratic times, that freedom was being restored to all. The Society was in favour of the change but there were concerns, aesthetic as well as economic. The surfacing chosen seemed almost too rugged, but gradually it weathered and became smoother with use. These streets in their new guise are now an accepted part of the scene.

Opposite, top: Inside the auction shed pigs go under the hammer at the Norwich Cattle Market, *c.* 1935. About the time this photograph was taken a total of 212,000 head of stock were sold here and sales amounted to over £1,250,000 per annum. The cattle market finally disappeared in the 1980s.
Below: The Cattle Market looking towards Barclays Bank, *c.* 1930.

Fair on the cattle market, *c.* 1930. Easter and Christmas on the cattle market meant time for the fair. Boxi
booths, tented shows of freaks, strong men and wild animals, helterskelters, toffee apples and kidd
roundabouts were just some of the fun to be had at these fairs.

The fun of the Cattle Market Fair in the early 1950s. In the austere postwar year the travelling fairs brought welcome colour and entertainment to the city.

orwich Cattle Market Fair, *c.* 1955. As time went on the fairs on the cattle market became larger and
ighter as steam-powered rides gave way to those driven by electrical generators and decked out with
ectric light bulbs.

Norwich City Cattle Market, 1960. For generations the Norwich Cattle Market by the castle was an integr
part of life in the city. On 25 June 1960 the last cattle market was held near the castle and the sales we
moved to the new purpose-built livestock market at Harford Bridges on the southern outskirts of the city.

Digging deep! Construction burrows down and cranes stand high when work was in full swing on the construction of Castle Mall in 1991.

Once a place of trade and public fairs, this green area is what lies atop of the Castle Mall today. An ope
green space for all to enjoy amid the hurly-burly of the city, sadly no fairs are held here – there simply is n
enough space. Consequently, the poor old Easter and Christmas fairs have suffered a somewhat itinera
existence since the construction of Castle Mall. *(Sarah Cocke)*

Opposite: Completed in September 1993, this is the interior of part of the Castle Mall. Costing £75 millio
within a total development cost of £145 million it is a multi-level shopping complex mostly situated und
seven acres of the old cattle market site. *(Sarah Cocke)*

Asda supermarket development. In the late 1970s and early '80s moves became apparent for th
development of the first out-of-town superstores. By 1981 concern was such that public inquiries were he
and the Norwich Society registered its clear opposition. In this first wave the majority were refused b
because the development of the new Norwich Sports Village was planned nearby, the Asda supermark
went ahead. The tide could only be held back for so long. As new housing developments push th
parameters of the city further across its surrounding hamlets the out-of-town supermarket has become
familiar feature all round the city. *(Sarah Cocke)*

8

The 1990s

Major Schemes & Change in the Office

The fire at the Assembly House, 12 April 1995. *(Sarah Cocke)*

The changes in the employment scene had continued with the closing of the Boulton & Paul factory on Riverside. That this long-established Norwich firm, with a romantic history linked to airships and aeroplanes and latterly more mundane things like wire-netting and windows, should close its city base, was sad in the extreme. The closure was the prelude to traffic and planning matters of the first magnitude. A site of about 40 acres, in several ownerships and uses and in planning terms considered a part of the city centre, was becoming available for redevelopment.

Also at this time Norwich traffic management was reaching an important stage. The crowning glory of the ring and loop system would be to complete the ring, the final phase of the inner ring road – briefly put, to connect Queen's Road with Riverside Road. The County Council, as highways authority, proposed a tunnel under Ber Street allowing the road to link with Rouen Road and cross the river by a new bridge over the River Wensum close to Carrow Road and then finish in a gyratory system with Rosary and Riverside Roads. The City Council thought this to be too destructive and came forward with its own scheme, after commissioning Malcolm Buchanan and Partners (a firm that knew Norwich traffic systems of old). This scheme picked up the line of the old ring road, or the ring road that should have been, and connected Martineau Lane to Harvey Lane. It was the City Council scheme that won the support of the Norwich Society. It disliked the destruction and the disturbance to residents that, in its view, the County Council scheme would have produced. Nor, remembering Magdalen Street and its forever-regretted flyover, did it want to see another part of the old city lopped off and placed in a sort of no man's land. For a frustratingly long period of time there was impasse; Riverside could not be redeveloped until the path of the inner ring road was known, and on that there was no agreement.

A public inquiry was held into the choice of route for the inner ring road and the Norwich Society gave evidence to it. A former city architect and a strong supporter of the Society, David Percival, undertook the task of putting the Society's views before the inquiry and the many weeks of listening to the arguments pro and con the County Council case. In the end the inquiry did not support either the county or city routes. The southern bypass was after all a major player in the scheme of things, and Riverside went ahead with a new road configuration within the scheme. It was an extremely busy time for the Society's traffic committee, chaired by Eric Sexton and planning appraisal, headed by Alan Couch. David Percival's contribution was of great value and, sadly, he died not long afterwards following an accident.

In 1991 there was major change, when Jean Ogden who had been secretary/organiser since 1964, decided to retire and Sheila Kefford was appointed in her stead. The 'office' of the Society moved the short distance from Waverley Road to Eaton Road. Jean had played an enormously important role over nearly three decades in building up the Society and was very much its public face. In replacing Jean, Sheila was undaunted by the size of the task and brought prodigious energy, with a capacity to learn quickly, to her role. Both these ladies, in their different ways, have been vital in maintaining the Society's reputation and influence within the city and beyond. Sheila came to office at a time when the whole tenor of local government was changing, particularly in places where, whatever their history, unitary status was lacking. Both city and Society needed each other on occasion. Sheila and the Society were honoured when she became Sheriff of Norwich, an ancient office she filled with distinction.

After all the doubts and uncertainties, Castle Mall opened in the autumn of 1993 (during a Society holiday in Jersey). It has since built up, with its diverse shops and a multiplex cinema, into a major contributor to the city's shopping facilities, and these have in recent years scored consistently highly in national lists. Not the least of the benefits of the Castle Mall has been the way it has restored dignity and scale to Timberhill. The Society was fully in support of the planning brief for this important old street and it is satisfying to see it free of the early postwar gimcrackery and with a worthy façade on both sides. Pedestrian priority has worked well and shops of quality have come to the street. Timberhill represents one of the happiest Norwich street revivals of recent times. The Society made its own pleasing contribution to the Castle Mall scheme; having carefully conserved the old Duke's Palace Bridge, it was passed to the developers who installed it as an impressive entrance to the underground car park.

Traffic and access to the city were matters never far from the Society's thoughts throughout the decade. Members had seen the success of such schemes in other cities such as Oxford, and so the Society was in the vanguard of those pressing for 'Park and Ride' to be introduced to Norwich. Although there was little enthusiasm in certain quarters at first, gradually the idea was accepted and the Norwich Area Traffic Strategy made provision for several sites around the perimeter of the city, of which that at the airport saw the first purpose-built interchange. A lengthy restoration of George Skipper's Royal Arcade, where the glory above ground was perhaps not matched by the state of the foundations, thoroughly deserved commendation. Commend it the Society did, marking its award by a notable stone plaque. Less happily, the Society became increasingly dismayed by the incidence of criminal damage and unruly behaviour in the city centre. In some areas of the city such as Bridewell Alley, constant damage to shops had begun to have an economic effect on streets of charm and individuality. A body known as City Centre Watch came into being, hosted and chaired by the Society, and with members drawn from traders, the police, the City Council and others, met regularly to discuss ways of combating growing problems. Solutions emerged as time went on, among them CCTV and a bye-law to prohibit the drinking of alcohol in the streets.

The loss of industry, following the trend of previous decades, continued with the closure of the Nestlé factory at Chapelfield. Established by the Norwich chocolate making firm of Caley's, by which name it had been known to generations of Norwich people, it had merged with Mackintosh, the Halifax toffee-maker, between the wars. Subsequent mergers saw Rowntree become the dominant name and then the giant Nestlé. It was this concern that followed a familiar pattern and considered the continuation of manufacturing in Norwich to be uneconomic. The decision came as Christmas approached and with the English Historic Towns Forum meeting in the city. The closure provided a vivid illustration of the changing face of our urban life. It also meant that a prime parcel of land, close to the city centre, was available for redevelopment. Plans were soon laid for a department store, other shops and a residential component. This, with the land made available by the moving of the hospital, meant much change in the southern approach to the old city.

The moving of the hospital was another contentious issue. The first proposals were for Norwich to have a second hospital with 'Norwich 2' in Colney Lane. The latter quite quickly became the only hospital, with 701 beds replacing about 1,200 at the Norfolk and Norwich and the West Norwich. The difference was to be managed by increased day procedures. The hospital had been on the St Stephen's Road site since 1770. Its central position made it accessible to those not using cars. The Norwich Society thought there was much to be said for retaining a central position but, in any event, wanted to carry out its traditional role of staging a public meeting for the matter to be discussed. The chairman of the hospital's governing body would not allow his senior officers to attend – he felt they had suffered enough. He did allow a Society representative to attend a meeting of the governing body to attempt to change the decision. The representative failed in this but was at least entertained by one member of that body asking memorably, 'What is the Norwich Society. They're not elected are they?' The new 'Norfolk and Norwich University Hospital' was built in Colney Lane, close to the University of East Anglia, which now possesses a medical school.

The Society celebrated two significant birthdays during the decade. To mark the seventieth in 1993 a tree was planted in Tombland and the seventy-fifth by a substantial financial contribution towards the replacement wooden bridge at the Plantation Garden. The latter was a splendid occasion with a garden party and exhibition and the bridge being declared open by John Timpson.

It was a decade of exhibitions and publications. Sarah Cocke and Jack Hall mounted an exhibition showing comparative photographs of each decade between 1923 and '93, with a large section on Norwich at War, a period of the city's life that well merited recall. This exhibition was very well received and made its way round the venues of Dragon Hall, Barclays (Gurneys') Bank and the Castle Mall. Sarah Cocke placed her skills as a professional photographer at the disposal of the Society and enabled it to build a fine library of scenes from city life. The war years were dealt with again in 1995 at an exhibition at Norwich Arts Centre, and in 1998 there was an exhibition at the Assembly House when the Prince of Wales attended during a royal visit to the city and met members of the Society. The Society published two books, *Norwich Bridges, Past and Present* and *The Captain and the Norwich Parks*, dealing with the work of Arnold Sandys-Winsch in the period after the First World War. Great efforts were made to interest people in their city by cooperating with the local press in competitions, such as the identification of city doorways, and history trails enjoyed by people of all ages.

In this last decade as the old century ended, one change in Norwich became very apparent. Even if the perception still lingers of Norwich as a quiet, rather staid cathedral city, the reality is very different. Nightclubs abound and parts of the city are as busy, perhaps busier, in the small hours as during the day. This, the night economy, has become very important to the city. At these times it is a city for the young, which brings some problems in its train, but there is something pleasing about so many young people finding their pleasure in the old town. Quite what R.H. Mottram and E.A. Kent would have thought of it all is a matter for conjecture. Might they not have taken it in their stride as merely another phase in a long, long story?

ERIC SEXTON

There is a type of man who, although enjoying success in his professional life, wishes to 'put something back' into the place where his endeavours, and his success, have been centred. Like his father before him, Eric Sexton is such a man. Eric was born in Norwich in 1920 into a family of shoe manufacturers. He was to marry Joan White, a daughter of another shoe-making family; indeed both families were very prominent within one of the great staple industries of twentieth-century Norwich. Eric was educated at Southwold, where fellow pupils included Michael Youngs and John Fielding. All three were to become Norwich magistrates.

It was Eric's father, Jesse Sexton, who was to establish the Sexton Arts Trust in 1951 to administer the Assembly House as a gracious meeting place for the people of Norwich. Eric was not only to inherit the business responsibilities of his father but also to be chairman of the Trustees for over thirty years. In the 1990s, when he could reasonably have expected to relax a little before handing over his responsibilities as chairman, the building was devastated by fire. With the Central Library adjoining having suffered a similar fate, Norwich had been dealt a heavy blow. It was a time for leadership and this was not lacking at the Assembly House. Although modestly claiming that the business imperative meant that restoration had to proceed with some despatch, Eric will admit that certain key decisions – and appointments – had to be made at that time. English Heritage was a stern taskmaster but they, and Norwich, should be pleased with the result.

Remembering that the Norwich Society had done so much in the 1930s to ensure that the historic structure was not lost to the city, it is fitting that the Society has had such a long association with the Assembly House. Swiftly back for meetings after the restoration, the Society has recently moved the administrator's office to the building. The administrator can now, quite literally, 'Keep an eye on things.' It was Jean Ogden who told Eric Sexton that the Assembly House, and he, must play a part in Society affairs. Eric came on to the planning appraisal committee in the days of Marion Leadsom, whose knowledge of Norwich buildings was immense and who kept immaculate records of every Society comment on planning applications. This was work that gave Eric great satisfaction. He also chaired the traffic committee and was a director of the Norwich Preservation Trust. He was chairman of the Society at the time of an Extraordinary General Meeting – extraordinary in every sense – when a packed Assembly House dealt with the question of eligibility for election to the executive committee. Eric pays warm tribute to the skill of the Society's president, the Lord Mayor, Barbara Stevenson, on that occasion.

Eric has retired quite recently from the chairmanship of the Assembly House Trustees' although the building, one suspects, is never far from his thoughts. Caring as he has for this much-loved Norwich venue for so long, and his work over many years for the Society, Eric may rest assured that he has indeed '. . . put something back'.

The Rosary Cemetery pictured in 1993. In the early 1980s this Gothic treasure was subject to sweepin[g] proposals for modernisation. The Norwich Society joined forces with other organisations and citizens [t]o robustly and successfully oppose such plans. The Rosary had been especially dear to one ex-Norwich Socie[ty] chairman, Ralph Mottram. Never morbid about the place, Mottram knew the site's history and i[ts] incumbents intimately. Even into his late seventies and eighties he could be found here trimming back weed[s] and carefully cleaning stones: a walk through the Rosary with Mottram as your guide was a meaningf[ul] walk through the history of Norwich and those who built the city we know today. *(Sarah Cocke)*

Opposite: Back of the Inns, 1993. A far cry from the row of little businesses which sprung up behind th[e] inns that fronted on Gentleman's Walk, this is the site of what was the old Norfolk Hotel, which spann[ed] between Back of the Inns and Castle Meadow. With a few adjoining buildings and the construction of [a] shopping area which passes under the road on Castle Meadow, this area has been transformed into part [of] the Castle Mall shopping complex. *(Sarah Cocke)*

The smoking, fire-gutted Norwich Central Library on 1 August 1994. For anyone who liked to read, it was a tragedy; for anyone with any feeling for their county's past, it was a nightmare. Thousands of books, documents and photographs from the local studies library and the 2nd Air Division (USAAF) memorial library were destroyed. An extraordinary effort from library staff, volunteers, historians and concerned people has helped to replace much of the collection, but inevitably some photos and manuscripts were simply unique and thus irreplaceable. *(Sarah Cocke)*

The fire at the Assembly House, 12 April 1995. Less than a year after the library fire another unthinkable conflagration occurred to gut the Assembly House. This magnificent concert and meeting venue, with its lovely restaurant so favoured for afternoon teas, rose again from the ashes, and was faithfully and painstakingly restored. It is open today with no obvious marks to show that a fire ever took place there. *(Sarah Cocke)*

A member of the Graf-Off team cleaning Pottergate underpass in 1997. In the 1990s the instances of graffiti and illegal fly posting in the city had become such a problem that direct solutions had to be sought. Representatives of the Norwich Society and Norwich City Planning Department visited Leicester where an initiative of three dedicated teams with high-pressure hoses were dedicated to the removal of graffiti. After a trial in Norwich was found to have positive effects on the problem, the Graf-Off team was permanently established: their sterling work is still being performed today. *(Sarah Cocke)*

The Nestlé site, 1998. After the loss of the brewing and shoe trades to the city, one of the greatest blows in recent years came with the closure of the Nestlé factory in 1994. Thousands of people marched to protest but the closure went ahead, 900 lost their jobs and decades of chocolate production at the site begun by Caley's came to an end.

The restored 'Forget Me Not' clock on the tower of St Michael at Plea Church, 1998. In the twentieth century the City of Norwich Corporation employed 'a clocks man'. For most of the time the position was filled by father and son members of the Steward family – both affectionately known as 'Josh' they looked after all public clocks in the city, including the churches. Sadly, expenditure cuts in the 1990s brought this valuable service to an end. The Norwich Society and Norwich Historic Churches Trust formed a group to deal with the problem, usually solved by fitting automatic winders on clocks. In 1997 this hard-working team also set about the restoration of redundant church clocks in St Clements, St John de Sepulcre, St Michael Coslany, St Michael at Plea, St Gregory and St Saviour. *(Sarah Cocke)*

orwich Airport Park and Ride, 1998. Always
ith a mind to alleviate traffic problems
ithout turning to potentially destructive road-
idening schemes, the Norwich Society sought
package of transportation measures to avoid
ongestion in the city. Learning from cities like
xford, park and ride schemes were seen as the
ay forward. Although there was little initial
nthusiasm from Norfolk County Council,
orwich Society pressure saw park and ride
hemes become an integral part of NATS
Norwich Area Transportation Strategy), and
ave been implemented to much acclaim.
Sarah Cocke)

RH Prince Charles is accompanied by George Richards, then chairman of the Norwich Society and Society
retary Sheila Kefford (right) at the 75th anniversary celebrations of the Norwich Society at the Assembly
ouse in 1998.

A view over the recently demolished site of the old Boulton & Paul factory site on Riverside in 1998. After years of decline the Norwich factory of Boulton & Paul, once internationally known as an airship and aircraft manufacturer, finally closed. This site, which totalled over 40 acres, held great potential for city and residential planners.

A part of the new development on Riverside in 2000. Careful thought was given to the development of the Riverside area. The scheme allowed for new routes for traffic, construction of new large retail premises, residential housing and entertainment premises such as nightclubs, restaurants and a cinema.
(Sarah Cocke)

e Millennium Bridge over the Wensum at Riverside in 2000. Built to mark the Millennium and the city's
sociation with its foreign twin city of Novisad, this structure is the first completely new river crossing in
e city for over one hundred years. *(Sarah Cocke)*

A modern view of St Stephen's Street. Once half this size, St Stephen's was a bustling city street where
seemed particularly cramped when two trams passed each other. In many ways the street cried out f
widening; after the bomb damage of the Second World War and the modernisation of the 1960s and '7
this was made possible and the street we see today was shaped. *(Sarah Cocke)*

St Peter's Street, 1993. Long
gone are the old inns and sho
and the City Hall takes its plac
on the right. In the distance
the view has also changed
recently. The trees and groun
car parking area seen here
have gone to make way for th
Forum and Millennium Plain.
(Sarah Cocke)

Conclusion

And Now . . .

The Forum and Millennium Plain. (*The Forum Trust Ltd*)

It is quite a short step from the site of the Curat House where the Norwich Society had its beginnings to the Assembly House where its office is to be found today, but a great deal has happened on the way. The Curat House looked out on to a crowded old city, with its cathedral and churches, the castle on its mound and the cattle market gathered around it – a place possessed of character and considerable beauty. The people who came together at the first meeting did not want the changes they knew were inevitable to destroy too much of the city they had known.

From the Society office at the Assembly House today it is possible to look out on to a different city, but still one that the founders of the Society would recognise. The castle is there on its mound and in the distance the cathedral spire shows above the buildings of the central city. The church of St Peter Mancroft has a new companion in the Forum, an impressive replacement – and rather more than that – for the Central Library lost through fire. Along Bethel Street and past St Giles' Church the founders would find that Norwich has a second cathedral, the great Catholic church of St John the Baptist given by the Duke of Norfolk, raised to cathedral status in 1976. All around, except those lost during the war, are still the old churches of the city. Some are no longer open for worship but they continue to hold their historic place in the Norwich scene. The founders would hear of a good regional airport and a university that ranks among the first twenty in England. Some of the founders would be disappointed at the changes in local government but relieved that the Crown had renewed the city's civic distinctions.

At the rear of the Assembly House, the founders would find that chocolate-making has been consigned to Norwich's past, with new shops and residences about to claim the site. A little further off, they could be told, more residential building will take the place of the old Norfolk and Norwich Hospital although the buildings along St Stephen's Road will survive. None of them would believe that Barclays Bank had succumbed to the wiles of Cambridge and had deserted the magnificent Gurneys' Bank on Bank Plain; nor would they enjoy hearing that Colmans was much reduced and that a large part of its site awaited regeneration.

What the founders of the Norwich Society would accept, if it were possible for them to return, is that cities do not, indeed cannot, stand still. Change brings regrets but also opportunity. The loss of industry at Riverside has caused an entirely new city sector, with a stylish new bridge, to come into being. The nearby former Reads' Flourmill and its immediate vicinity are shortly to be redeveloped. This and other enterprise is bringing fresh life to Conesford, after forty years of dereliction.

In the early 1930s J.B. Priestley came to Norwich as part of his *English Journey*. Priestley saw Norwich as something more than a mere provincial town, and not simply an old cathedral city. He saw it as 'an antique metropolis', a true provincial capital. He said his own city, Bradford, was more than twice the size of Norwich but somehow Norwich seemed the greater place. Priestley felt it was because Norwich had flourished as a city '. . . in the minds of men for generations'. He would have understood the aims of the Norwich Society.

In 1948 Arnold Kent and Andrew Stephenson in *Norwich Inheritance* were fearful that other than its buildings of renown, Norwich would have little to show in fifty years time. Those fifty years have passed but the worst fears of Kent and Stephenson have not been realised. One feels that Priestley would still give the city a nod of approval. A local authority that has cared, the Society, and their joint creation, the Norwich Preservation Trust, can all take their fair share of the credit. In spite of mistakes, to which mere humankind is prone, Norwich remains a city of which its citizens can be proud.

As for the Society, its founders would be pleased that what they so courageously began has been so well continued.

rial view of the demolition of the old Nestlé site in 2002. As we forge forward into a new century and a w millennium, changes are still taking place in Norwich. This view shows the extensive area of the apel Field Works of Nestlé's Chocolate Factory under demolition. The plans for the development of this a have involved much public consultation. Over the years to come battles will undoubtedly be won and t, but rest assured that the Norwich Society watches all the developments in our historic city as keenly as id when it began eighty years ago.

SELECT BIBLIOGRAPHY

Atkin, Malcolm, *Norwich: History and Guide*, Sutton, Stroud, 1993.

Ayres, Brian, *English Heritage – Book of Norwich*, B.T. Batsford, London, 1994.

Banger, Joan, *Norwich at War*, Albion Books, Norwich, 1974.

Cluer, Andrew and Shaw, Michael, *Former Norwich*, Archive, Attleborough, 1972.

Cocke, Sarah and Hall, Lucinda, *Norwich Bridges Past & Present*, The Norwich Society, 1994.

Hepworth, Philip and Ogden, Jean, *Sixty Eventful Years*, The Norwich Society, Norwich, 1983.

Kent, Arnold and Stephenson, Andrew, *Norwich Inheritance*, Jarrold, Norwich, 1948.

Nobbs, George, *Norwich City Hall*, Norwich City Council, Norwich, 1988.

——, *Norwich: A City of Centuries*, Macklow, Norwich, 1971.

Plunkett, George A.F., *Rambles in Old Norwich*, Terence Dalton, Lavenham, 1990.

Priestley, J.B., *English Journey*, William Heinemann, London, 1934.

Skipper, Keith, *The Norfolk Connection*, Poppyland Publishing, 1991.

Wicks, Walter, *Inns and Taverns of Old Norwich*, Norwich, 1925.

Young, John Riddington, *The Inns & Taverns of Old Norwich*, Wensum Books, 1975.

ACKNOWLEDGEMENTS

This book would not have been possible without the generous advice and assistance of the following: Sheila Kefford, administrator of the Norwich Society; Dr Richard Cock, who read the text and made many helpful suggestions; the staff of the Norfolk Records Office and Norfolk Local Studies Library; the chairman and council of the Norfolk & Norwich Archaeological Society; Malcolm Crowder, secretary and surveyor of the Norwich Preservation Trust; Peter Franzen and the staff of the *Eastern Daily Press*; Sarah Cocke who has done so much to establish the modern Norwich Society Archive; Sir Bernard Feilden; Eric Sexton; John Ogden; Janet Ede; Alan Sewell; Ron Fiske; the helpful and patient staff at the Assembly House; and by no means least, Mr Philip Armes, without whose generous loan of photographs this book would not have been so enriched.

The authors also wish to extend their thanks and love to their families for their support and forbearance throughout this project.